JOSEF STRAUSS

Genius Against His Will

A related title of interest

The Greig-Duncan Folk Song Collection
P. Shuldham-Shaw and E. B. Lyle

A related Pergamon Journal

History of European Ideas
Editor: EZRA TALMOR, *Israel*

A new multidisciplinary journal, established by a group of international scholars to study the history of the cultural exchange between European nations

Free specimen copies available on request

JOSEF STRAUSS

Oil painting by an unknown artist, 1865.

JOSEF STRAUSS
Genius Against his Will

by

FRANZ MAILER

Translated by

PHILIP G. POVEY

For the Johann Strauss Society of Great Britain

PERGAMON PRESS

OXFORD · NEW YORK · TORONTO · SYDNEY · FRANKFURT

U.K.	Pergamon Press Ltd., Headington Hill Hall, Oxford OX3 0BW, England
U.S.A.	Pergamon Press Inc., Maxwell House, Fairview Park, Elmsford, New York 10523, U.S.A.
CANADA	Pergamon Press Canada Ltd., Suite 104, 150 Consumers Road, Willowdale, Ontario M2J 1P9, Cana
AUSTRALIA	Pergamon Press (Aust.) Pty. Ltd., P.O. Box 544, Potts Point, N.S.W. 2011, Australia
FEDERAL REPUBLIC OF GERMANY	Pergamon Press GmbH, Hammerweg 6, D-6242 Kronberg-Taunus, Federal Republic of Germany

First English edition 1985

Library of Congress Cataloging in Publication Data

Mailer, Franz.
Josef Strauss: genius against his will.
Translation of: Joseph Strauss.
Bibliography: p.
Bibliography of Strauss's works: p.
Includes index.
1. Strauss, Josef, 1827–1870.   2. Composers – Austri
Biography.   I. Title.
ML410.S915M313   1985   785.4'1'0924 [B]   85–63S

British Library Cataloguing in Publication Data

Mailer, Franz
Josef Strauss: genius against his will.
1. Strauss, Josef   2. Composers – Austria –
Biography
I. Title   II. Josef Strauss. English
780'.92'4   ML410.S915

ISBN 0–08–026765–3

Previously published as *Joseph Strauss, Genie wider wille*
Franz Mailer. © 1977 Jugend und Volk Verlagsgellschaft
Wien-München

Printed in Great Britain by A. Wheaton & Co. Ltd.

Contents

Contents

Translator's Note

"His intention was to be an engineer – and he became a composer. Musicians called him 'the Schubert of dance music', yet throughout his short life he stood in the shadow of his more popular brother, the Waltz King, Johann Strauss."

Professor Franz Mailer has placed all who love the Viennese dance forms deeply in his debt. This first ever published biography of Josef Strauss does more than pay homage to an overshadowed genius of music, and gives us more than an insight into the everyday life of his family: it is a revelation of how Josef Strauss played a major role in the development of the waltz in particular, to a degree of sophistication and musical depth previously unknown and since unsurpassed.

Fate dealt harshly with Josef, and his own family were often hardly kinder. We are the beneficiaries of his musical legacy, and Franz Mailer's fascinating and often moving book cannot but serve to further that legacy's enrichment of our lives.

P. G. P.

I

Täuberln

p Joh. Strauss-Vater   Op. 1

By the time Josef Strauss was born, on 20 August 1827 in the handsome "middle-class dwelling house number 39" in the Vienna suburb of Mariahilf (now 65 Mariahilfer Strasse), the married life of his parents had at last become more settled.

The marriage of Maria Anna Streim, the daughter of a well-to-do innkeeper, to the rather free-and-easy fiddle player Johann Baptist Strauss was the result of a sudden passion which, during the carnival season of 1825, drove this pretty girl into the arms, and soon the bed, of the young musician who was living from day to day, careless of his poverty. Strauss was an orphan and, in addition to his activities in the then small orchestra of his friend Joseph Lanner, he found it necessary to give lessons to make ends meet. In the summer of 1825 he wanted to set off on a tour "to Graz and the Imperial Lands, to find work". With this intention he applied for a passport, but Anna Streim dissuaded him. She knew herself to be pregnant and was anxious to marry as soon as possible.

Strauss, three years younger than Anna, acquiesced. His legal guardian had the banns called promptly and the wedding took place on 11 July 1825 in the pleasant little Parish Church of Lichtental. The young couple set up their first simple home in a small house "Zur Eule" (The Owl) in the suburb of St. Ulrich and there, on 25 October 1825, the expected child arrived; a son. He was christened Johann Baptist, after his father.

The hastily contracted marriage started off better than

anticipated. Johann's guardian had to promise, in his official support for the marriage contract, that Anna would contribute towards her own maintenance by the production of womanly handwork. In the event, this turned out to be unnecessary. On 1 September Strauss ended the partnership with his friend and Principal, Lanner. Their quarrels, parting and at the same time reconciliation, were celebrated in typically artistic fashion with a waltz (by Lanner). Strauss now organized his own orchestra.

Within the walled city of Vienna and in the fast growing suburbs, there were enough proprietors of inns and other establishments prepared to allow concerts or music for dancing in their rooms and gardens to provide a living for both the "Blackamoor" Strauss and the "Flaxenhead" Lanner. Strauss dedicated his Opus 1, the "Täuberln" waltz to one of these landlords, Michael Deiss, and his Gasthaus "Zu den zwey Tauben" (The Two Doves) situated in the Palais Traunschen on the Heumarkt. As the exuberant young "Musikdirektor" responded to storms of applause by repeating again and again this charming piece, which was lacking in any strict form and really offered little more than a few short motifs gathered together into a round of melodies, he realized that he had achieved his first, but at the same time decisive, success. In November 1827, in the Gasthaus "Zur Kettenbrücke" (The Suspension Bridge) – situated in the Donaustrasse next to the old Dianabad – Strauss presented a further work; the equally well received "Kettenbrücke" waltz. With this he firmly established himself in favour with the Viennese, and on a par with Joseph Lanner. A "waltz contest" began, and it was only to end with Lanner's early death in 1843; unresolved and unresolvable.

The high pitch of the initial triumphs also accelerated the pace of the Strauss family's everyday life. They moved to a more spacious dwelling in Mariahilf. There, from the outset of his career before the public eye, it was possible for the nervous, effervescent, often dictatorial Musikdirektor to rehearse and work out his ideas in careful detail. His wife, possessing a natural musical talent, accompanied him with simple chords on her guitar which was rumoured in her family to be an heirloom handed down from mysterious, supposedly aristocratic, Spanish ancestors.

Josef was born into this idyllic situation. His mother had the leisure to give particular care and attention to her second child. Special care was indeed necessary, as little "Pepi" showed from earliest childhood the first symptoms of some brain damage that occasionally appeared to affect the spinal cord. The doctors were baffled; later they spoke vaguely of nervous depression and advised maximum care and plenty of fresh air. For the time being there certainly seemed no grounds for serious apprehension. Pepi developed normally; he was merely quieter and more reserved than his elder brother "Schani", who displayed his father's temperament, bordering on nervous hysteria and, in this restlessness, a tendency towards practical jokes.

By the autumn of 1829 at the latest, the somewhat cosy and relaxed life of the Strauss family was, however, irrevocably at an end. In the meantime they had moved house twice, and prepared for yet another removal to "Zum weissen Wolf" (The White Wolf), a house situated directly on the banks of the Danube. Father Strauss now gained a lucrative post of musical director at the famous establishment "Zum Sperl", in the Leopoldstadt district, which with its elegant ballroom and splendid gardens, was in those days rated as the most favoured pleasure spot for Vienna's middle-class society.

The appointment involved not only more work for the composer–conductor and increased tensions; Strauss directly encouraged and stimulated the reform of Vienna's musical life. In contrast to his friend and by then rival, Joseph Lanner, Father Strauss was no "Biedermeier".⋆ He was driven on by an

---

⋆ Biedermeier: from Ludwig Eichrodt's poems "Biedermaiers Liederlust" and subsequently used to describe not only that period from the Congress of Vienna 1815 to the revolution of 1848 but also a change which was reflected in the art and fashion of the period. All art forms were softened and furniture adopted clean lightly curved lines. Simplicity was its key factor and this was also extended to a description of human characteristics. Thus, to pleasant, respectable, broadly comfortable bourgeois people.

overpowering spirit of enterprise, typical of the era following the Napoleonic wars and the Congress of Vienna (1814/15). At that time, factories were springing up all over Europe, and mass-production became a reality. The machine age was just beginning and the continent was crossed by a network of railways. Johann Strauss had recognized with astonishing certainty the possibilities of this new industrial age, and he energetically began to take advantage of them.

During a concert Father Strauss did not suffer his musicians to go among the audience, music in hand, to make collections as he himself had done in Lanner's orchestra. He stationed a cashier at the entrance to the Gasthaus or garden in which he was performing, and levied an entrance fee of a few kreuzer. This was certainly a modest charge for a concert that offered besides dance-music, selections from the operas and even popular symphonic works in excellent performance. The cashier and the entrance fee however, set Strauss apart from the harpists and more casual musicians of the "Heurige" wine gardens.

Strauss now insisted on giving a title to each of his compositions. For every society ball, for each of his spectacularly arranged festivals, specially dedicated pieces had to be

Birthplace of Johann jnr. (now 15 Lerchenfelder Strasse).

composed and presented in as striking a manner as possible. The public could thus later identify individual works, and were encouraged to buy the music as soon as it appeared in print. Even though the carnival season balls and summer festivals followed one after another in quick succession, Strauss drove himself on to produce a continuous stream of new "dedications".

Strauss also recognized the possibilities of advertising and unhesitatingly exploited them to publicize his concerts and festivals as well as his printed compositions. In this, he found a like-minded partner in his publisher, Tobias Haslinger. As a consequence the editors of the Viennese press found Strauss to be a generous client and in return they provided rave reviews and highly complimentary articles as for example in the *Theaterzeitung*.

In view of these developments in the Strauss household it is hardly surprising that people began to speak of a waltz "business". The intensity of organization that went into the production of the dance compositions was revealed, almost casually, by Johann Strauss the son, when in 1887 he wrote in a foreword to the Complete Edition of his father's works:

> In those days one would often announce for a particular evening, a waltz, not one note of which existed in the morning. In such cases the orchestra would usually gather at the composer's home. As soon as a part of the composition was ready, it was prepared and copied out for the orchestra by assistants. A few hours later the piece was ready and, after rehearsal, was performed in the evening before a usually enthusiastic public.

Similar commentaries, by Father Strauss's contemporaries, indicate that the staff of assistants were by then capable of completing the product along the lines of an established pattern. Fundamentally, only one thing was required of the composer: that he should produce an idea, for the success of a piece created in this way was determined exclusively by the quality of this inspiration, this "idea"!

Now, at no time had Strauss, or indeed his rival Joseph Lanner, been lacking in musical ingenuity. Both men created, in their contrasting ways, a world of music for dancing and entertainment which was in harmony with the lifestyle of the people, accompanying their everyday lives and stimulating their celebrations. However, the important and striking role which Strauss and Lanner were able to play in the life of Vienna, particularly during the 1830s, can only be understood in relation to the unusual political situation of the day. Kaiser Franz I and his Chancellor, Clemens Fürst Metternich, wished to maintain peace among the peoples of the Danube Monarchy and, in particular, the inhabitants of the capital city and Imperial residence, Vienna. It was preferable that the people should be debating which one of the two rivals composed the more exciting, sparkling or graceful waltzes than that they should occupy their thoughts with, in the words of Kaiser Franz, "useless ideas of freedom and the already forgotten Paris revolution". Prince Metternich encouraged the press to give full coverage to more popular topics. The censors were thus able to undermine the "distasteful political talk" which was so disliked by Metternich.

In 1835, Kaiser Franz died and his eldest son, Ferdinand, ascended the throne. Ferdinand, known as "The Good", suffered from severe epilepsy, which occasioned a disrespectful joke among the Viennese: "Ferdinand der Gütige" was transposed as "Gütinand der Fertige" – ". . . the Finished". The principle of maintaining peace had by now been promoted to the level of State policy. Prince Metternich certainly raised no objections when, in this atmosphere of conscious exaggeration of the unimportant, both Lanner and Strauss were proclaimed as "Waltz Kings". Each of them proved to be thoroughly worthy of the title for by the time of Lanner's death the Viennese Waltz had already found its definitive form. Both Lanner's "Schönbrunner" (1842) and Father Strauss's "Loreley-Rheinklänge" (1843) are consummate works of art.

Father Strauss was not satisfied with being acknowledged only in Vienna. In 1833 he drew up plans for the tour which his marriage had previously obliged him to postpone. To begin with he took his orchestra to Pest, Vienna's twin city on the Danube. In the following autumn he went to Berlin, and on the way back home gave concerts in Leipzig, Dresden and Prague. Yet, as he found success and his dynamic personality evolved, so he became more remote from his family circle. Being a proficient business-woman, Anna tried at first to keep up with her husband. When, as the result of a powerful ice-flow, the Danube flooded its banks and forced the family to evacuate the house "Zum weissen Wolf", she organized the move with quiet efficiency in spite of having given birth to her third child, a little girl (Anna), only a short while before. Later, they found ideal accommodation in the spacious rooms of the house "Zum goldenen Hirschen" (The Golden Stag) in the Leopoldstadt. Here she established with her family, which had in the meantime been enlarged by the addition of another daughter, Therese, and a son Ferdinand (who died soon after), a new home which could also be used by the orchestral personnel for rehearsals.

Nevertheless, Anna Strauss had to recognize that her husband was becoming progressively more distant from her and the children. It was said that he often took to gambling until the small hours of the morning to relax his excited nerves after a strenuous evening's performance and indeed Strauss was subsequently punished for committing such an offence. Then there were rumours that the Herr Musikdirektor had found a "Gspusi" (girlfriend). Strauss denied it obstinately and his wife readily believed him, the more so as she was expecting another child. Yet when this last son, Eduard, was born on 15 March 1835, Anna Strauss knew for certain that she had been deceived. After several affairs, Strauss had finally established a firm relationship with a young milliner, about twenty-five years old, named Emilie Trampusch, and it particularly hurt Anna's pride to discover that the first child of "this Trampusch", a girl, was born only two months after her own "Edi".

All Vienna, at this time, took the side of Father Strauss. Although he freely admitted his affair with the buxom, not particularly intelligent but good-natured Emilie, and his paternity of the seven children who arrived at regular intervals (the last in 1844), none of his friends deserted him. Even at the normally so prudish Imperial Court it was conceded that he had been fettered by what was now seen as an over hasty marriage. Anna Strauss also eventually accepted that her husband should continue to live in the "Hirschenhaus", although in a separate apartment, and maintain his paternal authority over the children.

It was an armistice – everything soon appeared to be smoothed over, but the ten-year-old, already precocious "Schani" (Johann jnr.), saw the upset in the family as a catastrophe. He was deeply sympathetic to his mother's unhappiness and instinctively took her side although his father had been his idol, and as a musician was to remain so. He had always been determined that he too would become a Musik-direktor. Now he swore that some day he would outshine his father! That much he owed to his mother! Anna Strauss understood the thoughts and feelings of her eldest child and all her life she was to remember his loyalty. Josef, more intro-verted by nature than his brother, kept himself in the background. He was also devoted to his mother, and with his shy and tender affection repaid her for her care and attention in his upbringing. For this reason, he felt no strong bond with his father. He determined, above all, to become a good scholar and to bring home good reports from his first school in the Leopoldstadt and later the famous Schottengymnasium. This augured well for his future.

II

Freiheitslieder

Joh. Strauss-Sohn   Op. 52

Despite being "Trampusch's bed companion", as he was scornfully dubbed by his sister-in-law Josephine Streim (the stern yet popular "Aunt Pepi"), Strauss did not neglect the welfare of his legitimate family. In return, he wished to retain his right to determine the future of his three boys, although he was scarcely interested in the two girls. Originally, both Johann and Anna Strauss had shared the opinion that none of their sons should take up the uncertain and indeed strenuous profession of a "waltz-fiddler", nor become a musician of any kind. "But", recalled Johann Strauss the son later, with obvious satisfaction, "we had inherited from our parents the love of music, and that simply could not be restrained." In a frequently quoted recollection he is more specific:

> Living apart from us, father had little idea of what went on within the family. True, he allowed us, my brother Pepi and I, to learn the piano, but he thought that we were just tinkling at the keys in an amateurish fashion. However, we worked passionately at it, and I can honestly say we were both accomplished pianists. He had no idea of this.
>
> The rehearsals for his concerts were held in our flat. We boys listened attentively to every note, familiarized ourselves with his style, and afterwards played in duet at the piano the music that we had overheard, exactly in his spirited manner. He was our ideal. We were often invited to visit (respected) families and would play from memory, and to great applause, our father's compositions. One fine day, an acquaintance congratulated him on our success. He was not a little astonished. "Let the boys come over!" was his immediate decision. We crept with foreboding

9

into our father's room. In a few brief words, he informed us of what he had heard and ordered us to play for him. He had an ordinary upright piano; Pepi explained that we could not possibly play on such an instrument. "What!", he exclaimed, "you can't play on that?! All right then – we'll have the grand piano from the flat!" The grand was brought in and we played as well as we could, bringing out all the orchestral cues. Smiling, our father heard us through, and one could perceive the pleasure and emotion in his face. "Boys, I don't think anyone could play that better than you!" was all he said, but we each received a reward.

Through his characteristic diligence and tenacious perseverance, Josef Strauss subsequently turned himself into a virtuoso pianist. Johann of course, true to his intention, to which in the meantime he had also converted his mother, soon took up the violin. In this, he promptly came into conflict with his father:

> I took up the violin of my own accord. To enable me to pay my teacher, I gave piano lessons . . . My teacher told me always to practise in front of a mirror, so as to acquire an elegant bearing and good bowing technique, as elegance of appearance was indispensable to anyone who wished to perform in public. Well, I followed this teaching faithfully. One day, I stood in front of the mirror as usual and began to play; the door opened and in came my father. "What!" he cried, "you play the fiddle?!" He had no inkling of this. Purely by accident he had learnt that I wanted to become a professional musician, and there ensued a violent and rather unpleasant scene. My father wished to know nothing at all of my plans.

Father Strauss attempted to assert his rights as guardian, but Anna opposed him with the utmost vehemence. She began an action for divorce, and simultaneously laid claim to every penny of her husband's income from the Imperial Court and the Vienna City Authority. She even asked that Father Strauss's uniform, as Director of Music of the Citizens' Guard, should be put under lock and key. Strauss fled the "Hirschenhaus" in a rage: Johann Strauss jnr. however, could now realize his ambition to be a composer–conductor. His début took place on 15 October 1844 at Dommayer's Casino in Hietzing.

The first public appearance of the young Strauss was a great sensation for all classes of Vienna's population. Dommayer's small but elegant Casino was already full to overflowing before

"Strauss-Son" raised his violin for the first time in public, to play his graceful "Gunstwerber" and "Sinngedichte" waltzes. Everyone knew that with this début the son was demonstrating his opposition to the father, and the affairs of the Strauss household were once again the talk of the town. Furthermore, the young Strauss undeniably pleased the people. Since the death in 1843 of Joseph Lanner, Father Strauss had alone ruled the waltz business in Vienna. He now read in a report in the *Wanderer*, by the writer Franz Wiest: "Good night, Lanner! Good evening, Strauss-Father! Good morning, Strauss-Son!"

However, the enthusiasm of the Viennese for the young Strauss did not last long. The novice Musikdirektor soon found himself reduced to his true position in the entertainment world of his home town, Vienna. He surrounded himself with, as later the paper *Die Geissel* (*The Whip*) derisively wrote, "such a haze, as youthful as it was arrogant, around the 'sun' of his new status that he did not appear to notice the things which were happening outside this misty horizon." Nevertheless, it could not escape his attention that once again all Vienna supported his father, the "reigning Waltz King", against him, the "aggressive son". In 1846, the Imperial Court even bestowed upon Father Strauss, its conductor of dance music, the title of honour especially created for him – "Hofball-Musikdirektor"! The young Strauss very soon found himself forced out of the centre of things in Vienna and, beyond his own circle and age group, his only faithful followers within the capital were the Slav communities – the Czechs, Serbs and Croatians. When "Der fesche Schani" (the smart and stylish Johann), as he was already known, reacted to the pressures and isolation by giving free rein to his lively temperament, his reputation grew steadily worse. Ten years later, a postscript to a Police report addressed to the Imperial Court read: "Ever since becoming a Musikdirektor, he has been a rash, immoral wastrel"!

Through the increasing hardships of the eighteen-forties, "Schani" and his orchestra found they were no longer able to earn their living in Vienna and in the autumn of 1847 they were obliged to seek subsistence by means of an arduous and

11

extensive concert tour throughout Hungary and Transylvania, to Bucharest and Wallachia.

Josef Strauss remained aloof from all these goings-on; patiently and unerringly, he developed his many-sided talents. In the autumn of 1841 he had, together with his brother Johann, enrolled at the Polytechnic Institute, and in the following year (Johann having finally decided upon a musical career), completed his studies in technical drawing and mathematics in the Technical Department of the Institute. At the same time he began to take private tuition in ornamental and landscape drawing. In the academic year 1845/6 Josef chose a course in mechanical engineering, and passed the final examination "with the assessment – First Class". In consequence, he was employed in August 1846, to make architectural drawings, and received a reference stating that he had "shown such progress that he deserved recommendation to anyone".

A characteristic silhouette by the student Josef Strauss. The slender bridge joins "Zufriedenheit" (contentment) with "Preparedness for death".

While Johann Strauss jnr. limited himself exclusively to intensive work with the orchestra, Josef complemented his studies by taking an ardent interest in Vienna's fascinating cultural life, which was particularly rich during the years from 1844 to 1847. He regularly attended the Philharmonic Concerts which had been founded in 1842, and the illustrious festivals of the "Gesellschaft der Musikfreunde" (Society of Friends of Music). He heard the pianistic virtuosity of Franz Liszt and admired the musicianship of Clara Schumann. At the theatre, both Josef and Eduard became familiar with the works of Hector Berlioz and with the performances of celebrated prima donnas. At the "Theater an der Wien", appeared Jenny Lind, for whom Giaccomo Meyerbeer especially travelled from Paris and personally produced his opera *Vielka*. To this same theatre came the graceful Jetty Treffz, and at the Kärntnertortheater shone the petite Anna Zerr. At that time, Albert Lortzing took up residence in Vienna and introduced his "Waffenschmied" (The Armourer). In the Leopoldstadt, Johann Nestroy's puns and cutting humour were enthusiastically received and, of course, the Strauss brothers knew the young Franz von Suppé, whose operatic comedy overtures were popular concert pieces.

Despite such artistic attractions, life in the Danube metropolis became increasingly harsh and difficult. Large sections of the population, particularly the working classes, slid into penury. Thus the ground was prepared for the insurrection which broke out in Vienna, in March 1848, against the hated doctrine of Metternich. The fire of this generally felt enthusiasm succeeded in transforming Josef, the quiet retiring student, into a convinced revolutionary. Certainly, Father Strauss also made some initial concessions to the spirit of the times but he soon reaffirmed his stand on the side of the established order and, in August, he emphasized his true feelings with his famous "Radetzky March". Johann Strauss jnr. who returned to Vienna with a (Hungarian!) "Victory March of the Revolution" in his orchestral repertoire, joined the younger element and wrote a few pieces that were more humorous than warlike, such as the comic anthem with the title "Freiheitslieder" (Songs of Freedom) – originally called "Barrikadenlieder"! Only Josef Strauss resolutely took up arms and, as Eduard wrote in his "Memoirs", "marched on 26 October with the Academic Legion to the marshalling point of the army where he was placed in the firing line alongside the Nassau Regiment." When the dreaded "Seressan" troops of the Croatian Banus Jellačić were about to storm the Leopoldstadt, however, Pepi speedily left the battlefield. He hid his uniform in the chimney, and his rifle behind a clothes chest in the "Hirschenhaus", and retired to the Monastery of the "Barmherzigen Brüder" (Brothers of Charity). On All Saints' Day, a military patrol attempted to ferret out the "Studentsky" at his home, but with the help of three silver pieces "for a drink", mother Anna Strauss promptly succeeded in curtailing the hunt for her son.

In December, Father Strauss became concerned about the future of his wayward son, and ruled that he should become a soldier in the Pioneer Corps. Josef categorically refused:

> I could never devote myself to that profession, the more so as I would be of no use in it, would take no pleasure in it, and have never had the least desire for it . . . Let me stay where I am and who I am . . . do not tear me away from a life that can offer me so much happiness – I do not want to learn how to kill people but to be of service to humanity as a man, and to the State as a citizen. . . .

Josef saw his purpose in life quite clearly: he would become an engineer and architect. Nothing and nobody would deter him from that.

III

Die Ersten und Letzten

In the late afternoon on 22 September 1849, in the "Redout-ensaal" of the Hofburg, the Vienna City Council organized what was, considering the circumstances in which the city found itself following the brutal suppression of the revolutionary movement, an exceptionally splendid festival in honour of Field Marshal Radetzky. Two-hundred-and-fifty guests took their places at the sumptuously spread tables and the Strauss Orchestra had been engaged to entertain them, but the Herr Hofball-Musikdirektor, unexpectedly failed to appear and the new "Radetzky Banquet March", which he had announced, could not be performed. The assembly was not, however, unduly concerned about this.

That very same evening, the family heard about the events in the Hofburg. As Father Strauss had long since moved into the Kumpfgasse near the Stephansplatz with his mistress Emilie Trampusch, and the only contact with his wife was through third parties, cautious enquiries were made as to why Strauss was absent from the banquet. Eventually news came: the Herr Hofball-Musikdirektor had caught scarlet fever, while playing with one of his and Emilie's children, but he was already on the way to recovery. Josef and Edi wanted to visit their father, but were refused admission to the house.

Early in the morning of 25 September, an agitated man arrived at the "Hirschenhaus" and breathlessly reported a rumour that the Herr Hofball-Musikdirektor had died suddenly

15

in the night. Josef Strauss immediately made his way to the Kumpfgasse where he found the door open and the apartment, apparently vacated in great haste by Emilie and her children, in a state of devastation. Cupboard doors stood open, drawers had been pulled out and, in the ghostly half light of the early morning, Pepi eventually saw his father's body. A doctor who had already been called, arrived and entered on the death certificate that he had died ". . . from transmission to the brain of scarlet fever", aged 45 years. The authorities then had the apartment sealed. The inventory later refuted all contentions that Emilie Trampusch had completely stripped the rooms and left the body of her companion naked and uncovered. This malicious slander was, nevertheless, regularly revived.

Josef Strauss returned as quickly as he could to the "Hirschenhaus" with the news. Immediately, Johann and his mother seized the initiative: the dead man again belonged to his "legitimate family". Anna inserted the announcement in all the papers and, as funeral arrangements had already been organized by friends of the deceased, she arranged for a Solemn Requiem in the Court Chapel. Johann used all his influence, as if no dispute or rivalry had ever existed, to be recognized as his father's successor. At the same time, a spiteful campaign was launched against Emilie Trampusch: Josef Weyl, who was later to write the text of the "Blue Danube" waltz, even published a derisory verse about the unfortunate woman.

Just three weeks later, the path of the future was established. Strauss jnr. took over his father's orchestra and, at the same time, virtually all his engagements throughout Vienna. Only the Imperial Court refused his request to provide their ballroom music; preference being given to Philipp Fahrbach. This, however, was the one remaining obstacle and when, in the course of the next few months, it became known that "the Trampusch" was pregnant again, and this time could not name the father of the child, the last of the deceased's friends now changed their allegiance to his son. The woman with whom Father Strauss had lived happily for fifteen years, disappeared without trace.

The Viennese sincerely mourned the man who, as a principal violinist and conductor, had given them so much joy, so many happy hours. More than a hundred thousand lined the route as, following a funeral service in St. Stephen's Cathedral, he was borne to the Döbling cemetery to be laid to rest at the side of Joseph Lanner.

With the death of their Waltz King, virtually all of the mourners believed they were witnessing the end of an era. It was therefore a considerable and significant achievement that, in the course of the next few years, Strauss the son not only proved himself capable of assuming his father's role in Viennese life, but at the same time convinced the populace that the era of the waltz was by no means a thing of the past. Violin in hand, he showed them that the spirited dance, the elegant image of a cultured way of life, would remain alive as long as he played the music. He richly deserved their subsequent elevation of him to the position of Waltz King. In direct contrast to the extremely tense and nervously hectic pace of his brother's activities, Josef Strauss developed his many talents with characteristic calmness. During his first years as a student, he had already evolved and produced various educational aids which had found many grateful clients. He also made silhouettes, which were in considerable demand as presents. Furthermore, with accomplishments at his disposal, not only as a virtuoso pianist, but also as the possessor of a fine bass voice, Pepi wrote some remarkably pathetic and melancholy songs, mostly settings of his own texts, as well as some really demanding piano pieces.

Josef also tried his hand as a playwright, the material for his drama being drawn from a family legend. It was believed that his grandmother, Maria Anna Streim (née Rober) was descended from the Spanish aristocracy. As the daughter of a marquis who had the misfortune to have mortally wounded the Infanta(!) in an ill-advised duel, she had to flee her homeland with her parents. To avoid detection, "Marquis Rober" renounced his rightful title and took on the menial post of assistant to the pastry-cook in the house of the Duke of Saxe-Teschen, who was well-disposed towards him. The grief of his situation, however, brought about his early death. Josef enlarged upon this curious story – a pure invention – which he entitled "Rober" and became quite carried away with his enthusiasm for it, designing both scenery and costumes to accompany the text.

As far as was possible in these difficult times, Josef again took up his studies and also worked as a draughtsman. He travelled daily by the same route as a young girl named Caroline Pruckmayer, whom he knew through attending a language course. Now they met again and, between the student and the eighteen-year-old needlewoman working in a fashion salon, there was spun the thread of an increasingly passionate love. Caroline's mother (the girl's father had died shortly after her birth) would not at first even consider a match between her daughter and the "young man with neither money nor profession", but even when the Pruckmeyer family moved to a different suburb, it did not put an end to the love affair. Before long, Johann Strauss also began to visit the little house in Grinzing and so the situation became somewhat obscure when, in April 1851, Josef Strauss had to depart for Trumau in Lower Austria to undertake the supervision of the building of a stone dam in a brook known as the Triestingbach. Although he was an ambitious engineer, this parting from Caroline caused him to take an immediate dislike to the work in Trumau. Indeed, in his first letter Josef complained:

> My good, dear Linchen!
> I am far away from you. Even if I were to leave this place on account of you, just to be with you, I still could not see you for a whole day! I see you in my imagination, in front of me, I smile at you, I kiss you and press you to my heart . . . I love you with all the strength of my being . . . I seek my happiness only with you, for it lies within your hands . . .

A week later he began his letter as follows:

> Here I am in Trumau again, in my purgatory; in my penitentiary . . . I am cruelly punished, forced to stay away from Vienna, from you. I can hardly visualize your face. My stay in this place is terrible for me, the monotony of the environment, these blockheads around me – in short, I have had more than enough of this Trumau place. . . .

Josef's sketches from the "penitentiary".

Before long, Josef was tortured by anxious thoughts as to whether he could be sure of "his Lina's" fidelity. It had not escaped his attention that his beloved, like countless other women and girls in Vienna, was infatuated with his dashing and elegant brother Johann, who now occasionally took the opportunity to pay court to her. Sometimes Pepi could not suppress his jealousy: It made me very sad to hear that you were in the Volksgarten; I would not have believed a word of it had I not been told by letter.

In the Volksgarten his brother Johann had on 15 July, presented a festival concert!

On 30 July, Josef concluded what had originally been scheduled as a full year's work, and returned to Vienna. He undertook the construction of a machine-shop, and his place of work was situated in the immediate neighbourhood of the salon where Caroline was employed.

In the spring of 1852, a happy and optimistic atmosphere reigned in the "Hirschenhaus". During the carnival season, "Jean" (Johann) had made his first appearance as conductor of a ball within the Imperial Court, thereby realizing the highest position previously held by his father. Pepi (Josef) was negotiating with an eminent architect who wanted to entrust

19

him with the building of two large dwelling-houses. Furthermore, he planned to complete his studies with a course in dam construction and to gain his engineering diploma. Pepi also designed a street-cleaning machine and submitted the plans, with detailed explanatory notes, to the city authorities.

By the late autumn of 1852, the situation had completely changed. Johann Strauss returned thoroughly exhausted from a concert tour of Germany that had taken him as far as Hamburg, and soon afterwards fell ill with a "nervous fever". The doctors actually feared for his life, and with good reason. They prescribed a lengthy convalescent holiday as being essential to avoid a relapse. His mother was in despair; a similar state of exhaustion had precipitated her husband's early death. If the large family was to survive however, the "waltz business" had to continue and, come what may, with a Strauss at the head of the orchestra. There was only one solution: Pepi must step into the breach as conductor.

For some time, Josef resisted the family's vote, but there being at that moment no alternative, he gave way. He made one stipulation however: he had never mastered the violin (which at that time was indispensable to a musical director) and, unlike his elegant brother, had not practised in front of a mirror. He would take over the direction of the orchestra, but only on an interim basis. The family agreed. Even if Pepi only posed as conductor, appearances would be kept up and the "business" saved.

The outcome was that on 23 July 1853, in the old "Strauss Headquarters", the "Sperl", Josef Strauss made his début as conductor of the orchestra. "The unavoidable has happened", wrote Pepi to his fiancée Lina, Johann was able to depart for Bad Neuhaus for his cure, but he forgot to provide the traditional new piece for the church festival in the Vienna suburb of Hernals, so his brother was also obliged to deputize as composer. Josef wrote a genial waltz, but he gave it the title "The First and Last" – and he assured anybody who was prepared to listen: once, and never again.

"Interimskapellmeister" Josef Strauss.

Father Strauss   Mother Anna

First ball in the Sophiensaal (1846) with the Strauss Orchestra in the background. Father Strauss conducted. His sons later played for dancing in this still existing hall.

Josef Strauss's youthful song-cycle: neither text nor music shows the happy characteristics of the waltz. The compositions of his youth remained in the family's possession and escaped destruction. Of the 121 sheets of manuscript however, many are now in private collections and therefore not accessible for research.

Caroline, the love of his life.

IV

Mairosen

p Op. 34

Throughout the summer months of 1853, life went on agreeably enough for those Viennese remaining in the sun-baked capital. Although on 18 February, an attempt had been made on the life of the young Kaiser Franz Joseph, it was eventually decided in the Hofburg to relax the martial law that had been in force throughout the monarchy during the past five years, and on 1 September it was completely lifted. That unique carousel, synonymous throughout the world with Vienna and the joy of living, gradually began to revolve again. The ravages of 1848, the revolutionary year, were repaired: in the suburbs, they were enthusiastically building and the number of inns, entertainment halls and pleasure parks was rapidly increasing.

In August and September Josef Strauss, conducting the orchestra in lieu of his brother, reflected upon the situation with customary thoroughness. More establishments meant, inevitably, a greater number of balls and concerts. A permanent relief for Johann was consequently desirable but the family's financial situation was by no means firmly established. On one occasion Anna Strauss was obliged to seek a hurried loan and, then again, the somewhat careless Johann had to thank his publisher, Carl Haslinger, for not insisting upon some repayments of a debt. So, it was better to stand on one's own feet. Josef had no difficulty in carrying out his task of maintaining the "waltz business" in full swing while keeping the competition at bay. Neither the young August Lanner, Joseph Lanner's son, whose début in March had been rapturously acclaimed by his father's followers, nor Philipp Fahrbach, certainly proficient but lacking a personal touch with the public, constituted a danger. Yet the daily commitment of performing in public rooms and halls frightened him. Had the doctors not recommended he should take things easy and get plenty of fresh air? Why did his mother urge him to spend his nights in the stifling atmosphere of gas-illuminated dance halls?

Other aspects of his new activity however were decidedly tempting. The musical life of Vienna had not yet recovered from the setback of 1848. The Philharmonic Concerts had been discontinued, the reorganization of the "Gesellschaft der Musikfreunde" was proceeding very slowly, and the era of the dilettante orchestra was indisputably past. In the preceding months, it had been left to the Strauss Orchestra to introduce the music of Richard Wagner, and for the winter season Johann prepared a performance of the *Tannhäuser* overture, as yet completely unknown in Vienna. These were the plans which particularly interested Josef Strauss!

But at this time Josef had been required to make his début composing an old fashioned Viennese waltz because people at the church festival in Hernals preferred to dance in Ländler fashion (Austrian country dancing). Josef had not found it difficult to imitate the style but, as he had not received any lessons in harmony or counterpoint, was obliged to bluff his way through the introduction. Nevertheless he managed to capture the intonation and impression of an old school Viennese waltz so well that his composition "The First and Last" had to be repeated six times. The papers were generous in their praise:

> His waltz abounds in freshness and dash; in that electrifying effect which appears to be exclusive to the Strauss family. (*Wanderer*)
> These latest blossoms of the dance are positive proof of the brilliant talent of Herr Strauss, and we allow ourselves the pleasurable hope that this composition will not be his last. (*Theaterzeitung*)

It now occurred to Josef that it would be a good idea to further his musical studies. He therefore applied to train "in the

principles of thorough-bass and composition" under Franz
Dolleschall, Professor of Harmony and a qualified proprietor of
a school of music. In addition, he took violin lessons with Franz
Amon, the principal violinist of the Strauss Orchestra. "Interimskapellmeister" Josef Strauss did not attract much attention
in the summer of 1853. To begin with, the Spanish dancer
Pepita was thrilling the Viennese populace, and furthermore,
from 23 August onwards the entire monarchy was engrossed in
only one other topic of conversation: as the newspapers
expressed it – "the news is released of the engagement of Elise
Amalie Eugenie, Duchess in Bavaria, with The Emperor Franz
Joseph, in Ischl . . ."

In mid-September Johann Strauss reappeared, fully recovered, fiddle in hand, and "re-kindled the old spark in his
orchestra". No one gave any more thought to that pallid young
man who, conducting with the baton, had commendably
bridged the gap during his brother's temporary absence.

In the carnival season of 1854, Johann Strauss was more than
ever the centre of interest. He dared to allow a Wagnerian tone
to infiltrate some of his dance compositions. This excited the
public and the critic, Eduard Hanslick, went so far as to apply
the term "waltz requiems" to the "Novellen" and "Schall-
wellen" waltzes, dedicated to the Juristen (lawyers') ball and
Techniker (technicians') ball. This expression was quickly
spread around the city and was subsequently often to be used
against the Strauss brothers.

Josef Strauss did not appear as conductor, either during the
carnival season or in the spring. At this period his own health
was not at its best but when Johann left for a rest-cure in
Gastein, Josef willingly resumed the direction of the orchestra.
He began by presenting a new waltz, "Die Ersten *nach* de
Letzten" (The First *After* the Last) which appeared to indicate
that he had at least decided to continue composing but no
sooner had Johann returned to conduct the orchestra, at the end
of July, than Josef withdrew completely. His letters speak of
"eye trouble" and violent headaches.

The seal was not finally set upon Josef's future until 1855. In spite of the Crimean War between on the one side, the Western powers England and France allied with Turkey and, on the other side, Russia, Europe amused itself to its heart's content. The Danube Monarchy had remained neutral and within its capital the number of balls and festivals was greater than ever. Even in St. Petersburg, the fact that the Allies had assembled their armada on the Baltic Sea was not allowed to disturb the customary pleasures of the populace. The directors of a railway company, who were responsible for the operation of an excursion line from the Russian capital to the village of Pavlovsk, some thirty kilometres away, paid a visit to Austria in search of a new Director of Music. Although the palaces of the Tsar (now Puschkin) and of the Grand Duke (Pavlovsk) were situated along this line, it never for a moment occurred to anybody to support the rail service. Consequently, the management of the terminus station which was situated in the middle of a huge park, provided facilities during the summer for the presentation of attractions such as balls and concerts – "in the Vauxhall".★ If these events were well attended, then the railway must also show a profit!

As previously mentioned, the directors of this railway company sought a Director of Music who would possess a capacity to draw the public in great numbers to Pavlovsk. The attraction of the previous conductor, Joseph Gungl, was expended. In casting around for a successor to Gungl – who came from Berlin but was, by the way, of Austrian descent – the name of Johann Strauss came to mind. He did not need to be asked twice. This lucrative undertaking was exactly to his taste.

It seemed obvious that Josef should in the meantime deputize for him in Vienna, but still Johann hesitated. To begin with, in February 1855, he permitted his now twenty-year-old youngest brother Eduard, who besides training for the diplomatic service had also taken music lessons, to make his début as a harpist. He

★The term "Vauxhall" was a reference to the famous pleasure gardens that flourished in London from the mid-seventeenth to the mid-nineteenth centuries. In its Russian transliteration, "Vauxhall" has become the word for a railway terminus. (P. G. P.)

then made a drastic reduction in the number of Josef's engagements, both for the carnival season balls and the spring concerts. Johann suddenly had doubts as to whether Josef was the right man to give his (Johann's) works the required effect. Furthermore, it occurred to him that his brother's compositions might eventually prejudice his own! The publisher Carl Anton Spina had already approached Josef with a proposal to publish some of his dance pieces. Josef left the decision to the family. As Johann himself was however contemplating a change of publisher (Schott beckoned temptingly from Germany!), and was not entirely confident about the Russian engagement, he delayed his brother, combining some half-hearted concessions with certain strong reproaches. Thereupon, Josef gave rein to his annoyance:

> Dear Jean!
> From this, your last letter, I gather that you were in a hurry to finish it and catch the post. I thank you for enabling me to enlighten Herr Spina today – it is as I had expected – nevertheless, I had not thought you capable of such inconsistencies. If you will allow me, I will analyse your letter. Firstly, if you believe that no other publisher (*in loco*) except Haslinger can pay this amount, you should not be too quick in giving notice or breaking the contract. "H." is aware of this and, knowing that he pays well, treats you thus because (apart from the contract) he is also obliged to come to your aid in the event of your weakness or difficulty. These are the fruits of your having allowed him to dominate you too much.

Having fully debated in his letter, the question of his attitudes towards the publishers Haslinger and Spina, Josef goes into the attack:

> What is this rubbish that you talk about independent interests and egoism? Where is the egoism in a deplorable situation where one presents oneself to the public as a stop-gap, and encounters an auditorium made up of indifference and apathy. My function is of an interim nature; a substitute. As such, my accomplishment is that of an "also-ran" – I must devote myself to this occupation if the business is not to go under. This thought is uppermost in my mind, and is my incentive. I know of no other motives. Have I ever thrust myself into the role of conductor? Did I push myself to the fore when I was staying in the country last year? Who called on me in the first place? For me, the cessation of public appearances

29

Josef Strauss

In the summer of 1855, Josef wrote to Johann, then in Gastein, making his position crystal clear.

represents no threat or, at the least, no harm. My love of music does not show itself in 3/4 time, neither do I feel a call for it. I am therefore quite prepared to lay down the baton when you arrive. . . .

As a result of this letter, Johann Strauss gave in, once and for all. Josef, who had only shortly before been prepared to resign his position, could now think about the systematic building of a career as composer and conductor. He was once again required to provide a waltz in the established Viennese manner (a "Flinserln") for the Hernals church festival, but this time he surrounded his routine dedication piece with a whole series of further compositions. The spell was broken; the cornucopia of his inexhaustible ideas and inspirations began to gush forth. In the early summer of 1856, Johann made his first journey to Russia, and Josef appeared before the public, leading the orchestra with the violin. August Lanner was dead, Fahrbach had become a military bandmaster, but Josef had immediately to assert himself against keen new rivals. Yet, in the spring of 1857, when he opened the first Volksgarten festival with the waltz "Mairosen", Josef was already the reigning Prince in once more sunny Vienna!

V

Brennende Liebe

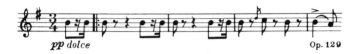

pp *dolce*   Op. 129

During the first summer of his exclusive directorship, Josef
Strauss set about changing and broadening the orchestra's
repertoire. Veterans in the orchestra had, since the legendary
days of "old" Strauss, been used to performing popular operatic
pieces along with the latest dances at the various soirées and
garden concerts. Even symphonic works had been presented,
flexibly adapted to be acceptable to the public, but Pepi was
now determined to venture much further. He exploited the well
known weakness of the Viennese for musical novelty by
presenting, in the Volksgarten, an "extraordinary festival" in
which he followed scenes from Wagner's *Lohengrin* (at the time
still unknown on the blue Danube) with the tone-poem
Mazeppa by Franz Liszt, heard there for the first time. Liszt, the
much reviled exponent of "new music" who had only just come
under attack for "daring" to direct a Mozart festival in Vienna,
sat happily among an audience of more than two thousand and
was well satisfied with the performance of his work.

  Josef Strauss was well aware that as violinist-conductor he
could never emulate the sheer magic and fascination of his
father; unlike his brother Johann, who was then in Russia and
who had proved himself from the very first day by transporting
the public into realms of enthusiastic delight at his concerts and
balls in Pavlovsk. For his own part, Pepi could see but one
prospect: at the cost of renouncing the further development of

all other talents and abilities, he would have to be as comprehensive as possible in demonstrating his "love of music". On the one hand therefore, he planned widening the orchestra's repertoire to include master-works of contemporary opera, and the "futuristic" music rejected by the critic Hanslick and his circle; and on the other hand, he planned the further development of the waltz as a "symphony in three-quarter time", for which the music of Wagner and Liszt quite obviously provided the inspiration.

Although in the summer of 1856 Josef worked zealously at his studies, he was as yet in no position to realize his plans for such compositions. Thus he contented himself for the time being with working more carefully upon the "old-fashioned" Viennese waltzes and lively, striking polkas, towards which he had been under the circumstances already motivated. The press once more encouraged him on the occasion of a "Festival of Old Vienna" at the "Sperl". The *Wanderer* reported:

> This composer, who has gained such rapid and universal popularity, performed his latest waltz, entitled "Die guten alten Zeiten" (The Good Old Days), a very melodious, spirited and brilliantly orchestrated piece, to the greatest applause.

With his compositions for the carnival season, Josef was less successful. He was working in the shadow of his brother and the greater experience of the elder, who had after all a head start of nine years, was at that time clearly apparent. There were also considerations of business' policy. Neither Johann nor the publisher Haslinger, who in the meantime had signed contracts with both brothers, showed interest in promoting Josef's carnival season compositions. In the winter, Johann was to be given clear preference.

Josef did not resent this. He was, in any case, excitedly awaiting the forthcoming spring because he had at last succeeded in obtaining Frau Pruckmayer's consent to his marriage with her daughter. The girl had long since realized that the happy-go-lucky Jean regarded her merely as one of many "acquaintances" – and her mother finally withdrew her opposition to the match with Josef. He had already planned, as a wedding present for Caroline, a composition in which for the first time he would introduce his further development of the Viennese dance form in a "Concert Waltz". He achieved his plan punctually. Two days before his wedding to Caroline Josepha Pruckmayer, on 8 June in the Parish Church of St. Johann in the Leopoldstadt, Josef presented his beloved with the waltz "Perlen der Liebe" (Pearls of Love). Three weeks later, in the Volksgarten, he played this exacting work which, with its bold harmonies and far-reaching melodic lines, represents even today a criterion for orchestras and conductors. But this time he waited in vain for an echo in any of the papers.

Disappointed, but for the moment not disheartened, Pepi picked up the threads of the daily routine, and when the Hernals Church Festival came round again, he was able to celebrate two successes. One of these was "Fünf Kleebladl'n", a waltz of the popular type; the other was a quick polka with the English title "Steeple Chase". The question now inevitably arose: was Pepi born to be merely a Viennese "popular" musician? An interesting comment appeared on 3 March, 1858 in the *Theaterzeitung*:

> While Johann Strauss follows predominantly in his father's footsteps, Josef is decidedly inclined towards Lanner's style. His waltzes in particular, express the same geniality, freshness and happiness that is so characteristic of Lanner.

Josef could therefore have taken life easily. To be Lanner's successor, was excellent for one's reputation and equally so for business. What would others not give for such an assessment? But Josef Strauss wanted more than that. He ventured on a fresh attempt: shortly following the birth of his baby daughter, named Karoline after her mother, he sketched another "symphonic waltz". He named it "Ideale", and presented it to the public on 15 June 1858 in the Volksgarten. This time, the critic of the *Theaterzeitung* was present to comment:

> The performance of the new Concert Waltz, "Ideale", was accorded the most splendid success. The piece departs from the usual waltz form in

that it moves in perfectly pure rhythms, that the melodies are most carefully constructed and are embellished with rich instrumentation. In this work, Strauss has proved that he is thoroughly conversant with musical construction and composition, that he understands how to use subtle combinations, turns of phrase and inter-weavings to their fullest extent. The work itself is a little *chef-d'oeuvre*. The reception was tumultuous.

Even if one is sceptical about the reports in the *Theater-zeitung*, on the grounds that its critics were usually "obliged" to attend benefit concerts, and were therefore prepared to comment favourably, this precise wording seems curious. It could be that in the "Ideale", Josef had extended or even split wide open the established form of the waltz. But this conjecture cannot be proved; the manuscript is lost, and the publisher, Haslinger, did not want to know about experiments. Two Concert Waltzes by Johann Strauss, "Gedankenflug" and "Schwärmereien", which undoubtedly were inspired by Josef's ideas, were failures and for this reason Haslinger also discouraged Josef. None of the "new style" waltzes or other concert pieces that Pepi later submitted (e.g., the Ode "An die Nacht", the Concert Waltz "Klänge aus der Ober- und Unterwelt", or the "Fantasie für Orchester") appeared in print.

Josef Strauss resigned himself to the situation. Being reproached that such compositions would not help the business, he did not even try to fight for his "Ideale". As a conductor, and increasingly an orchestrator and arranger, he turned his attention even more decidedly towards the task of introducing works which should have already been known in Vienna. As the witty journalist Ludwig Speidel had stated in the *Wiener Zeitung* on 10 February 1858, "Schubert (lay) still to a great extent buried, and while Mendelssohn is played to the death, his great rival Schumann as yet scarcely appears on the surface." Admittedly matters improved when, through the energetic initiative of the conductor Carl Eckert, the Philharmonic recommenced their concerts, and the "fiery spirit" Johann Herbeck intensified the activities of the "Gesellschaft der Musikfreunde". It was Josef Strauss, however, who in addition to Wagner's *Lohengrin* and *Der fliegende Holländer*, also introduced *Tristan und Isolde*, *Rheingold* and *Die Meistersinger von Nürnberg* to Vienna.

In the early summer of 1860, Josef Strauss presented excerpts from *Tristan* for the first time and, from May 1861, drew further attention to the work with new arrangements. These were heard, as Eduard Strauss attested in his "Memoirs", by Richard Wagner himself, who expressed his approval. It was not until November 1862 however, that the Vienna Court Opera attempted to produce *Tristan und Isolde*, and almost immediately discarded it as being impossible to perform!

Similarly, Josef Strauss championed Giuseppe Verdi, towards whom the Viennese critics bore even more animosity than to Wagner! He then added to the repertoire, compositions by Schumann and Schubert. It is therefore understandable that the German composer Peter Cornelius, on his visit in March 1861, found Josef Strauss to be "the more cultured musician of the two (Strauss brothers)". Such was the general opinion at that time.

Josef was not one-sided in his approach; he did not give his support only to operatic and symphonic music. From October 1858, as the light and comic operettas of Jacques Offenbach became known in Vienna, Josef presented the audiences at his concerts, after each première in the Carltheater (which was then under the direction of Johann Nestroy), with corresponding pot-pourris and quadrilles. Only in the case of *Orpheus in the Underworld* did Johann Strauss make the first move.

Within the world of Viennese dance music Josef had, by the summer of 1858, caught up with his brother. Before his first summons to conduct for the Court at the Palace of Schönbrunn he had completed in quick succession his master works: "Moulinet-Polka" – a dainty miniature tone painting and "Wiener Kinder" – a classic waltz; all composed in one effort from the Introduction to the last note of the Coda. Then, being elated by the general praise that his productions received from the Archduchess Sophie and her guests, he composed an especially lively and volatile waltz for the Hernals Church

37

Festival, entitled "Flattergeister". The principal melody of this dance was immediately converted into a popular Viennese ditty, sung everywhere to the dialect words – "Wann i amal stirb, stirb, stirb" (When once I die, die, die). Could there be more poignant recognition of Pepi, than that his merry tune should be associated with the ever-present, latent and mournful elegy of the Viennese?

During carnival time and especially in the summer of 1859, the awareness of war-like altercations in Northern Italy, which were to end in the breaking up of the Danube Monarchy, weighed heavily upon the mood of the capital. The "business" declined noticeably. Johann Strauss resolved nevertheless, with the support of his mother, who was still particularly indulgent towards him, to reorganize the family concern. In Pavlovsk, Johann had fallen in love with the capricious Olga Smirnitzki, and for the first time had made serious plans to marry. In the spring of 1860 however, when the girl wrote to him: "Do not condemn me. I will be brief. I have been engaged for two weeks!" – he by no means despaired, as he had earlier prophesied would be the case. He plunged with even greater passion into an association with the singer Jetty Treffz, seven years his senior, who had given up her successful career and was living with the wealthy Baron Moriz Todesco.

With his work, Johann exercised the greatest caution. In the carnival season of 1861, he permitted Eduard to conduct the orchestra at balls, and on 6 April 1862, to make his debut as "Kapellmeister" in charge of the orchestra. He thereby indicated his aversion to Josef again, quite openly, and instructed that only Eduard would present his (Johann's) compositions. In July, he gave his poor state of health as the reason for returning prematurely from Pavlovsk to Vienna. Again he wanted Eduard to replace him, but this time his mother put her foot down, and sent Josef to Russia.

Josef Strauss was furious at being suddenly torn away from his well ordered activities, and at being separated from Caroline. Furthermore, it was not until he arrived in Pavlovsk that he heard that Johann had only dashed back to Vienna so that he could marry Jetty immediately! "Do you all know about this?" he asked in amazement. He was consoled by a promise that he could hope for a good income from the Russian engagements for the next two summers. Johann cheated his brother however and, after returning to Vienna from the honeymoon, renewed his old contract.

Josef no longer had the strength to make fresh demands. The fulfilment of his duties in Pavlovsk had exhausted him. "I can once more mop my brow, and let them make me an errand boy again", he wrote home with resignation. He then composed a mazurka, and wrote above the music, "Brennende Liebe" (Burning Love). Was Josef thinking of his Caroline, or making an ironic allusion to his brother's sudden impassioned interest in marriage. One cannot say, for the commentary to this work, the explanation of this title, he kept to himself.

In the summer of 1862, Josef Strauss had to exchange the Viennese pleasure grounds, the "New World" (for which he wrote his "Neue-Welt-Bürger" waltz) for Pavlovsk near St. Petersburg, where he gave concerts at the Railway Terminus (top picture).

41

K. K.
Volks-Garten.

In den für die Winterfaison abgeschloffenen Räumen

Sonntag den 17. Oftober 1858

FEST-CONCERT

zum **BENEFICE** des

J. Strauß

unter Mitwirkung eines

Männerchores von 30 Stimmen.

Hierbei befonders zu bemerken:

1. **Flattergeifter**, Walzer von Josef Strauß. **2. Waldröslein**, Polka-Mazurka von Josef Strauß. **3. Quadrille** (neu zum erften Male) von Josef Strauß.

Ferner:

„An die Nacht,"

Tongemälde für Chor und Orchefter von Josef Strauß (neu zum erften Male.)

Duett und Finale aus der Oper „Der Fliegende Holländer", von R. Wagner (neu).

(Hier noch nicht gehört.)

Die Auführung des Tongemäldes „An die Nacht" erfolgt gegen 6 Uhr.

Die Programme werden an der Kaffa ausgegeben.

Anfang 4 Uhr.   **Eintritt 20 fr. CM.**

Findet auch bei ungünftiger Witterung ftatt.   **Josef Strauß.**

A typical Josef Strauss programme: a new piece by Wagner, three new dance pieces and the (lost) tone-poem "An die Nacht" (To The Night).

42

Jetty and Johann. To please his wife, the Herr Hofball-Musikdirektor grew the side-whiskers in 1863.

Josef in 1865, twelve years after his début as Kapellmeister. The effects of illness and overwork are apparent.

VI

Dynamiden

pp   Op. 173

Josef's intention to introduce a new composition "Freudengrüsse" at his first concert on returning from Pavlovsk in 1862,
did not ease the situation at home. The family was so unsettled
that order had to be restored in the "Hirschenhaus" before Josef
could take up his fiddle and perform his exceptionally spirited
and elegant waltz of "joyful greetings". Johann returned from
Italy just as exhausted as he had been in August when he
departed for his honeymoon. This "honeymoon" in Venice had
in fact become a rest-cure, and Jetty had begun married life as
her husband's nurse. Unlike Caroline, Jetty had no desire to be
integrated into the great Strauss household and she now urged
Johann that he should be paid out his savings with a view to
their leaving the "Hirschenhaus" as soon as possible. She also
let it be known that her husband's neuralgia necessitated as
much care and attention as possible and that the doctors had
recommended that, for the time being, Johann should give up
composing. Josef immediately forgot all his chagrin and loyally
set to work composing the dedications due for the carnival
season.

    The plan to open the season with a concert in the fashionable
Winter Garden of the Dianabad did not materialize however.
Eduard, the "arrogant Benjamin" of the family, known to the
Viennese since his début as "der schöne Edi", had quarrelled
with the lessee, and in consequence this distinguised establish-

ment was lost to the orchestra. Furthermore, this represented the second such incident; the first having occurred in the summer at "Weghuber's Kaffeehausgarten". There was nothing left for it but to return again to the "Sperl", which had been for some time in steady decline. It was not a tempting proposition because audiences at the "Sperl" were mainly interested in being amused and this inevitably lowered the standards of the concerts. One could not be choosy however, if one wished to stay in business. The competition of the numerous well-trained military bands became more noticeable from year to year while the number of "civilian" orchestras was rapidly diminishing.

On 9 November 1862 therefore, Josef Strauss appeared at the "Sperl", leading the orchestra and playing only the "popular" items of those he had composed for Pavlovsk: the polka-mazurka "Brennende Liebe", the quick polka "Vorwärts!", together with his special dedication, the delightful waltz "Freudengrüsse", and a jolly "Japanese March on Original Chinese Melodies" that he had written in connection with the first ever appearance of a Japanese Delegation in St. Petersburg. The more valuable fruits of his summer's work, among them several symphonic sketches, remained unheard. Haslinger did not publish them, and they remained unknown in Vienna.

Only with difficulty was mother Anna Strauss able to restore equanimity within the family. Harmony became all the more necessary when, on 8 January 1863, Eduard also married; and now at least ten people – Johann and Jetty for the time being included – depended upon the income from the orchestra! Within a short while Johann had withdrawn from the scene as a composer; he produced just the one waltz, "Leitartikel" (translatable only as Leading Article) for the first ball of the influential press association "Concordia". Consequently Josef had, for the first time, to carry the main burden of producing novelty pieces for the entire carnival series. He acquitted himself of this duty with good results, feeling proud of the fact that he was needed. For a students' ball, the proceeds of which were to finance a holiday project, he wrote a quick Polka "Auf Ferienreisen" (Off on Holiday); a piece that even today remains a "Reisser"! (a hit!). At a benefit ball in the Sophiensaal, he and his brothers provided a highly amusing carnival joke when they, although themselves convinced "Wagnerites", poked fun at the *Ride of the Valkyries*!

In February, having humbly petitioned once again, Johann Strauss received the long-desired title, "Hofball-Musik-direktor" (Director of Music at the Court Balls). The price, as it were, was that from then on he had to undertake to play only at Court, or for the balls of the nobility, and restrict himself, at the very least, to concerts in the Imperial and Royal Volksgarten. Thereby he had given up the claim to be, like his father, "Vorgeiger aller Wiener" – First Violin of all the Viennese. In this situation his brothers had therefore to step into the breach for as long as possible in order to cover the whole entertainment scene in Vienna. In the spring, Johann and Jetty travelled together to Pavlovsk, this time more for relaxation than to work. During the course of the summer however, there developed from an apparently insignificant origin (Strauss felt that he had been cheated over the settlement of an account), a deep-rooted conflict with the publisher Haslinger and his wife. The situation eventually reached such a state of reciprocal antagonism that it could not be bridged. (Eduard later placed the blame for this development on Jetty.) Haslinger's tactics to persuade his Viennese colleagues against doing business with the Strauss brothers met with a counter-attack: Johann applied for a licence to be a music-dealer, and rented modest premises on the Kohlmarkt. As a consequence the publisher Spina was able to offer contracts, at first to Johann and Josef, later also to Eduard, which within a few years made him a wealthy man!

But Haslinger did not stop there. In November 1863, he introduced the very young Carl Michael Ziehrer as a competitor. At first this counted for nothing; despite all the aid afforded him by the publisher, the shy "Michi" was unable to challenge the Strauss brothers as a Musikdirektor. Later however, after Josef's early death and Johann's defection into the camp of the operetta composers, Ziehrer succeeded in becoming Vienna's most popular Kapellmeister.

Josef Strauss

Johann Strauss   Josef Strauss

Eduard Strauss

In the "Carnevalsrevue" of 1864, Johann played six new pieces, Josef
nine and Eduard three – eighteen new dances in barely six weeks. (In
1867, the "record year", the number was twenty-five.)

In the Strauss household, the development of events was followed at first with some anxiety. Only Josef rebelled against the tactics of the family. It did him no good; his mother, still as ever the heart and soul of the business (neither Caroline nor Eduard's young wife Marie, dared to interfere with her judgements), severely upbraided him. Instead of considering his reproaches, she grumbled, "I can't help it if you don't like the taste of our meat!" Josef dutifully submitted.

The year 1864 started with an unexpected turn of events. Jacques Offenbach had promised the Viennese journalists a dedication waltz for their second ball, and had suggested the title "Abendblätter" (Evening Papers). Johann Strauss was immediately invited to compose a complementary piece on the theme "Morgenblätter" (Morning Papers). The outcome was a "waltz contest", on 12 January in the Sophiensaal, between the Parisian and the Viennese composer. The verdict, withheld out of courtesy on the evening of the ball, was given a few days later when both works were publicly performed in the Volksgarten: the victory undoubtedly belonged to "Morgenblätter"! But the Strauss Orchestra proved itself chivalrous: in February 1864, they presented with particular enthusiasm, the music of Offenbach's opera *Die Rheinnixen* (*Water Nymphs of the Rhine*), which had been rejected by the Kärntnertortheater. The Viennese derisively joked about the title – "Rein nix" (purely nothing!) but the brothers Strauss held the work in high regard.

The few festivals that took place in the summer of 1864 were overshadowed by the unpopular campaign, in alliance with Prussia, against Denmark. The Strauss brothers fulfilled their "patriotic duty": before his departure for Pavlovsk, Johann presented his "Deutscher Krieger-Marsch", and *en route*, in Berlin, his "Verbrüderungsmarsch". Josef, just as superficially, paid homage to the Austrian Commandant in Schleswig with a "Gablenz-Marsch", and finally greeted the returning troops with an "Einzugsmarsch". All three brothers donated the proceeds of certain compositions and summer productions to a fund for crippled soldiers. During these months, however, each had his own personal problems to solve.

Johann's recovery made very slow progress. Josef nevertheless made his first cautious attempt to break loose from the closely-knit family circle. Until then, all his efforts to find an impresario who would negotiate engagements for him in, for example, Paris or London had come to nothing. When Johann heard about such plans he determined, convinced of his brother's inability to stand alone, to frustrate them. By that time however, Josef had succeeded in finding an entrepreneur in Breslau, who promised to organize an orchestra and find him a concert hall seating 3,000. Full of enthusiasm, Josef signed a contract with him, to take effect from October 1864.

The prospect of following Johann's example at least once, and of being able to celebrate a triumph far from Vienna so uplifted Josef that, in the midst of his routine summer compositions, he produced two works which once again clearly demonstrated his diverse and far-reaching talents. At a festival concert in the Volksgarten on 9 September 1864, he played in succession the waltz, "Dorfschwalben aus Oesterreich" (Village Swallows from Austria), and the polka-mazurka "Frauenherz" (Woman's Heart).

The pastel colours of the "Village Swallows" waltz reflected a literary subject. The Hungarian-born writer August Silberstein, with whom Josef Strauss had been friends for some years, had published a volume of village tales, of which a critic for the theatrical journal *Zwischenakt* is quoted as saying: "They reflect the deep feeling and the cheerful humour of our country life, animated by figures of grace and vigour. The book is already in every drawing-room." Josef Strauss had also obtained a copy of the volume, "Dorfschwalben aus Oesterreich", and reading it was inspired to a harmonious sequence of well blended waltzes. An introduction, in which a Ländler melody hovers above a characteristic folk-music accompaniment, closes as a charming sound-picture with a gently chirruping waltz motif, which in turn leads into a string of melodies which could almost be derived from Austrian folk-lore, had they not been the invention of Josef Strauss's creative and sympathetic understanding. At no time did the composer indulge in mere nature-worship; his inspiration came firmly from the grass-roots of folk-music.

With the "Dorfschwalben aus Oesterreich", Josef Strauss returned once again to the "Ländler style" waltzes that he had been required to play at Unger's Casino in Hernals. In the meantime, those spaciously constructed establishments had been divided up and new proprietors of the diminished "Lokal" had adopted the slogan: "cheap beer rather than expensive music". But now Josef Strauss took his art form to the almost completed Vienna Ringstrasse and, with his experienced artistry, improved upon the motifs. A new type of waltz was created which his brother Johann was not to make use of until four years later with his "Geschichten aus dem Wienerwald" (Tales from the Vienna Woods).

The polka–mazurka "Frauenherz" is also a little tone-poem, rather than a dance. From the beginning of his career as a composer, Josef Strauss had made a habit of illustrating certain characteristics of the ladies, in little pieces mostly based on the polka rhythms. We have a "Naive", an "Amazone", a "Kokette" and "La chevaleresque". Now, in honour of his tenderly loved wife Caroline, Josef drew up a kind of musical balance-sheet, a gallant analysis of *all* women's hearts; and the sensitivity with which he achieved this is admirable.

On 9 October 1864, Josef gave a farewell concert in the Volksgarten, and then travelled to Breslau. On All Saints' Day he was back home again. He let the newspapers believe that the tour had been highly successful, but in his letters one reads differently:

> The hall is fine, it holds however, not 3,000 people as has been said, but 800 to 1,000. The man who has assembled the orchestra was here, we have spoken together and if all goes well the first concert will be on Thursday.
>
> After two performances I herewith describe to you the whole business. I have a very poor orchestra, which severely limits my repertoire. If the manager doesn't co-operate I shall leave straight away.
>
> I am having a break for six days, as Breslau is swamped with concerts etc. this week, which puts me at a disadvantage. If all goes well, I shall

come out of this with my travelling expenses and perhaps my Savings Bank papers. Do not reproach me . . . what does Mama have to say? On Tuesday I still have to give a farewell concert from which, however, I do not intend to claim any profit. Jean has not arrived. . . .

Thus the attempt to break loose from the family miscarried.

Following his return from Breslau, Josef made an attempt, not in keeping with his normally shy and far from aggressive personality, to compensate for his lack of success as an organizer and "star conductor" by putting even greater effort into those areas which it had been his intention to fulfil ten years previously. He accepted with composure Johann's insistence that Eduard should go to Pavlovsk in the coming spring for the first half of the season. It was certain that Johann himself would not be able to travel to the Neva in April; the "state of nervous exhaustion", which the doctors regularly confirmed but which could not be alleviated, prevented it.

The energy with which Josef Strauss now set about the fulfilment of "his programme" can be appreciated from the repertoire of his concerts and the ball-calendar for the year 1865. Hardly a week passed without the presentation of a new pot-pourri, a transcription (of songs by Schubert and Schumann, movements from Beethoven's sonatas, concert pieces by Liszt, Berlioz and Schumann) or a new arrangement from an opera. For the "Nobelbälle" of the 1865 carnival he prepared dedications which, while respecting the established form of the waltz, clearly approached his ideal in their melodies and harmonies. For the medical students he wrote a piece with the title "Herztöne" (Heartbeats) which began with a nervous palpitating waltz motif, suggesting more of a ghostly vision than the beginning of an "enchanting, intoxicating Viennese dance". For the Industrialists' Ball, Josef composed a waltz which, by its original title alone, "Geheime Anziehungskräfte" (Mysterious Powers of Magnetism), almost directly provoked his latent mystic belief in sinister supernatural forces which, to his mind, were concealed behind the plausible realities of life. Yet before writing down the first note, Josef transcribed the title into the language of his own poetic style – as "Dynamiden". For the introduction, he then composed a visionary tone painting. A soft opening call awakes with romantic sensitivity, a feeling of yearning; a forceful climax compels it to unfold into full flower. A cautious, restrained passage now leads into the waltz, which again begins very softly as if sounding from a distance; a soaring, swinging motif eventually opens out into the dance, but immediately sinks again; it rises once more, appears to weaken, but is propelled forward on the powerful rhythm of the accompaniment. The melody shifts to the minor key, but finally lifts out of its melancholy to a conclusive and brilliant triumph!

In his "Täuberln" waltz, Father Strauss had presented a pleasant succession of eight-bar motifs neatly set in a row; his son now extended the vision of his "Dynamiden" across 42 bars, and, following a complementary passage of twice 16 bars which was again in boldly painted tone colours, he repeated the broad arch. It was architecture in sound, which sounded strange enough in the dance-hall. But by that time, the public of the Nobelbälle had learnt not to be surprised by Strauss waltzes. The traditional concept of "*die* Walzer" (the walt*es*, i.e. chain of waltz tunes) now became modified as "*der* Walzer" (the waltz): as the compositions took on an unbroken homogeneity so did the language appropriately adapt itself. By then, moreover, the public were prepared "even in the ballroom, to listen to the first performance of a waltz without dancing, and thereby to show respect for the composer". The *Neue freie Presse* specifically pointed this out in a report of 1866: "This is a Viennese speciality of the most outstanding kind". Richard Strauss later showed that such compositions have their place not only in the ballroom – his opera *Der Rosenkavalier* contains a soaring motif very similar to that of Josef Strauss's "Dynamiden".

As if exhausted by the production of his genial visions for the carnival season of 1865, Josef suddenly collapsed at his writing desk and, despite the fact that medical care was immediately to hand, remained unconscious for several hours. The attack had been preceded by violent headaches. The doctors again spoke merely of "nervous excitement" and "congestions" as being a "sign of exhaustion", and recommended that Josef should take a holiday. Nevertheless, he did not leave until Eduard had returned from Pavlovsk to look after the "Vienna branch of the business".

In the spring, however, Josef Strauss was more active than ever. Immediately following the Vienna Philharmonic's first Schubert concert, he increased the repertoire of the Strauss Orchestra with the Overture to *Rosamunde*. Also in the Vienna suburbs, on the occasion of the much delayed Munich première of *Tristan*, he once again presented three excerpts from that opera. Schubert's influence, as well as Wagner's, eventually made itself felt in Josef's most precious waltzes. During the carnival he had dedicated his "Actionen" to the Lawyers, but now it was his intention to point out that his real world lay elsewhere – and accordingly he wrote above his new score, the title "Transactionen" as it contained a tone-poem which again burst open the established framework of the classical Viennese waltz. Again he spanned a great arch of daring harmonies, interwoven themes and swinging self-willed rhythms. The transitional step to the "symphonic waltz" was reached but not yet crossed. This time, however, Josef departed for his holiday immediately after the première and without awaiting the reactions of the press; not that there were any – the only "transactions" in demand were those at the stock-exchange.

VII

Wiener Leben

Op. 218

The holiday which Josef Strauss took on medical advice in August 1865, was his first relaxation since returning from the country in the autumn of 1854. His wife, who with varied success had often suggested that Pepi should go walking in the Prater or the Vienna Woods, accompanied him. They were both (in contrast to the rest of the family) assiduous walkers, and even ventured on the ascent of the Traunstein, near Gmunden, which at that time was still something of an adventurous undertaking. This climb, on which incidentally the rather inappropriately clad Caroline got blisters on her feet and they had to carry the little dog that went with them, was described by Josef in a rather amusing letter:

> . . . we made our way up a rocky path, dangerous because facing the Traunsee it leads up steeply to a coppice with a brook. The stream runs, uninhibited, across mountain and valley, peak and chasm; below, spectacular depths with waterfalls; above, pine trees, fir trees, rocks and stones, which threaten to come crashing down at any moment. If anyone had seen us, from nine o'clock until half-past-twelve, with a clear sky, a temperature of 30 degrees, clambering up parched and panting, they would have thought that we must be making a million. . . .

Josef, who in the spring had seemed in such a poor state that his friends were apprehensive about his appearance, allowed himself only six weeks' relaxation. Then, worries about the Vienna business drew him back to lead the orchestra. On 17

September 1865, at the "Neue Welt", he took up his burdensome duties again. The irascible, and at times dangerously quarrelsome Eduard was not to be trusted! Even Johann had, in the meantime, become aware of this. As his substitute in Pavlovsk, "der schöne Edi" had only succeeded in alienating the elegant audiences, rather than attracting them to the concerts. Annoyed, Johann wrote home:

> Eduard was supported only by the Pavlovsk women and young boys – the box-office takings remained in very poor shape and therefore the directors of the Railway Management, despite all the exultation (from the women-folk), were completely apathetic. Their goodwill could only be won if it rained money. . . .

As Johann did not intend to return to Russia in the following summers he tried, in a sudden departure from his previous attitude, to use his influence in establishing Josef as his successor. But it was now much too late for this. In Pavlovsk, they had already decided that it was time for a change and had engaged a new Musikdirektor from Hamburg.

Thus in 1866, the Danube Monarchy's fateful year, all three brothers shared the direction of the summer and winter concert seasons in Vienna; the first and only time in the orchestra's history that they did so. As the chronicler Friedrich Uhl emphasized, in one of his famous "columns" (on the day of Josef's reappearance), the "world-wide reputation of the Strauss Orchestra" thereby became enhanced. Such a co-operation could certainly not be considered as being practicable for the future however, and it can be seen from a single glance through the cash book that this ideal situation could not be viable. To be sure, the number of attractive establishments had increased from year to year. On the Ringstrasse, ceremoniously opened on 1 May 1865, the Volksgarten café had found a counterpart in the sumptuous "Blumensaal" (Floral Hall) of the "Gartenbaugesellschaft"; in the Leopoldstadt, the fine "Dianabadsaal" joined the "Sperl", which was then in decline; in the Fünfhaus district, the enterprising Carl Schwender successfully converted a dilapidated cow-shed into the vast "Colosseum" pleasure centre and at the same time, his existing "Bierhalle" and his

Einnahmen p. Jahr		Ausgaben p. Jahr	
1862	5670 20	5260	
1863	5901 25	5498	80
1864	5546 40	4843	
1865	6044 60	5149	
1866	5223 20	4346	40
1867	6917 40	5708	60
1868	6924 –	5700	
1869	5572	5668	

Josef Strauss kept carefully detailed annual accounts. Deducting expenditure from income, he was left with very little profit!

summer garden "Neue Welt" had complemented the small but highly esteemed "Casino Dommayer". Yet, in none of these establishments, parks and "Gasthäuser", was it possible for a concert-giving orchestra to make a reasonable income; the music was still regarded as supplementary to the food and drink, and the Musikdirektors had to be suitably modest if they wished to keep their situations. Fiddle playing had become a "penny in the hat business".

The entries in the cash-books accurately verify however that, in all the years, and despite the constant change of conductors, the drawing power of the orchestra in Vienna hardly suffered at all. Right from his début, Eduard Strauss had astonished and impressed the public with his imperturbable confidence. Josef gradually made up for the lack of outward elegance which had at first given him a painful inferiority complex, as he increasingly came to be regarded by the Viennese, and the ladies in particular, as an archetypal "romantic artist". His earnest, dark eyes, the high pale forehead and the full sensual mouth, underlined the force of his personality. "Pepi may lack style" they said, "but he compensates for it by being interesting!" His industrious nature and also his courage were recognized everywhere. Josef now ventured to do something which Johann, throughout his life, was never prepared to consider – he entered into controversy with the press. It so happened that the *Vorstadt-Zeitung* contended that Josef Strauss adopted unfair methods by which to oppose his rivals. Without seeking legal advice, Pepi took up the cudgels so energetically and with such skill, that the influential journal was compelled to withdraw.

Josef Strauss permitted himself only one caprice: of all places, he could not stand the Volksgarten, even though this elegant salon in the centre of the Ringstrasse's "green island" attracted the kind of public that appreciated the most sophisticated programmes. Josef wrote to Herr von Szabó, the lessee of the Volksgarten establishment, a letter which, despite the amusing style, conveys his annoyance:

> There are two things that I must most earnestly beg of you. The first is this: that you will have the goodness to fit a lock and key to the entrance door of the conductor's dog-kennel, as the public repeatedly come to this door and force it open despite the barbed hook. Our articles of wearing apparel etc. are thus laid open to the public gaze and consequently tend to disappear.
>
> The second is this: the rain comes straight through the roof of the kennel and therefore the conductor can never be dry in E.W.*
>
> I did not have the pleasure of seeing you after the concert yesterday, with regard to your inclinations about accepting my suggestions. Yesterday's concert produced 120 gulden. Acquaint me then with your final decision, so that we can settle our business to our mutual satisfaction, in harmony and goodwill, gentleness and good temper, humbleness and tolerance. Farewell! Tyrant!
>
> Strauss

Now it may be said that at least one of these virtues was temporarily lacking on both sides, as the orchestra withdrew from the Volksgarten from March 1861 until May 1862. Later, of course, they reigned again for many years in this much-favoured rendezvous of high society.

It is also interesting to take a look at the books of the publisher Haslinger. They show conclusively that Josef's compositions were continually in demand even if, in the first decade of his career, he had not attained the sales record of, for

---

*Presumably "Elendem Wetter" – miserable weather! (P. G. P.)

example, his brother's "Annen-Polka". The fees that he received could hardly be called princely. From 1860, the publishers allotted Josef Strauss 150 Austrian gulden for a waltz, 90 gulden for a polka, 30 gulden for a march and 100 gulden for a quadrille on original themes. (Quadrilles based on operas and, later on, operetta motifs fetched only 90 gulden!) From 1862, Josef also obtained 100 gulden for a polka. The number of compositions that the publishers committed themselves to accept on these conditions was limited and the works passed into their exclusive possession. The Russian publishers in St. Petersburg paid somewhat better, and Carl Anton Spina also raised the fees of the Strauss brothers. He could, nevertheless, for a single payment of perhaps 200 gulden, find himself the possessor of a world-wide success such as "Morgenblätter" or "Dorfschwalben aus Oesterreich". Composers of dance-music had at that time no claim to a percentage of returns or authors' royalties!

Even when all sources of income were reckoned up, profits from the "Strauss Orchestra Concert Organization" yielded absolutely no prospect of supporting three families plus mother, sisters and staff, no matter how hard they worked. Jetty Strauss had accordingly, immediately after her marriage, begun to encourage her husband to break loose from the family. She urged him to give up the waltz business and compose operettas. "He is not aware of the pressure, so it all proceeds easily for me," she wrote in a candid letter. Johann at first resisted but Jetty did not give in; so cleverly did she contrive the matter that he ultimately followed her advice. Moreover, Josef Strauss also appears, at least in passing, to have toyed with the idea of writing folk-plays or composing operettas. The announcement, published in several newspapers, that he had signed a contract with the Carltheater was not denied, and in fact a sketch for a folk-play in three acts with songs was found among his papers after his death. It carries the title – "Eine wahre Wienerg'schicht (von Schottenfeld)" (A True Viennese Tale – from Schottenfeld), and there is no reason to suppose that he was not the author.

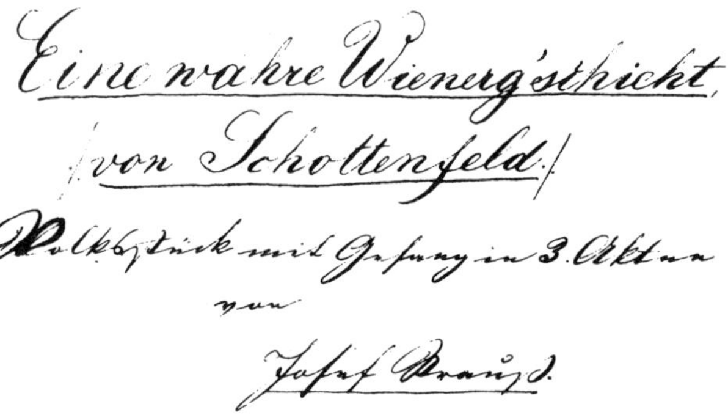

[handwritten manuscript facsimile]

"A True Viennese Tale – from Schottenfeld"

In the autumn of 1865, as the Strauss brothers began to prepare the dedications for the forthcoming carnival season, Johann proposed to give up composing "problematic material" and return to the "classical waltz". In January 1866, it transpired that Princess Pauline Metternich, wife of the Austrian Ambassador to France, had taken over the patronage of the Industrialists' Society Ball in the Redoutensaal because the profits were to be donated to her projected "Deutsches Hospital" in Paris. Although Josef was responsible for this ball, and had already composed his stirring "Deutsche Grüsse", Johann at the last minute also contributed a waltz, and a "classic" at that: the "Wiener Bonbons". This again stimulated Josef to compose a dedication to the influential Princess Metternich, the polka-mazurka, "Pauline". The piece however did not please him (or her?) and, when in April 1866 the brothers visited Paris to introduce their works personally, Josef wrote a second "Pauline-Polka".

With this, a new competition began once again between two Musikdirektors on Viennese soil, similar to that which had taken place between Lanner and Father Strauss, except that this time – and this is without parallel in musical history – two brothers opposed one another as rivals while at the same time working together in perfect harmony. Previously, Johann and

Josef had, from time to time, come to an understanding that on special occasions they would write a few works together ("Vaterländischer Marsch", "Hinter den Coulissen", "Monstre-Quadrille"). Now each, in turn, endeavoured to answer the other's master-work with a corresponding composition of his own.

In the preceding years, Josef had without doubt taken the artistic leadership. Johann, having initiated the return to the "classical Viennese waltz", now began to determine the direction for the future. Josef immediately followed suit. On the one hand, it was obvious that, so far as the public were concerned, Johann's "Wiener Bonbons" was more of a hit than Josef's "Transaktionen"; on the other hand, Josef knew he was now capable of creating every imaginable type of waltz. His artistic potential was at least as great as that of his brother.

During the carnival of 1866, which was hardly affected by the growing conflict with Prussia, the Strauss brothers achieved a record for new compositions. In the "Carnival Revue" of 18 February, seven new pieces by Johann, nine by Josef and five by Eduard Strauss were played, one after the other, in the Volksgarten. The public were enraptured by this flood of waltzes, polkas and quadrilles, and on 19 February the *Fremdenblatt* reported:

> . . . an enormous crowd attended this concert. Under the direction and hearty encouragement of the Strauss brothers, the musicians blew and bowed their instruments with such vigour and unity that, despite the African heat, few listeners left their seats and those that did were constantly replaced by crowds of new arrivals. It was a wonder that the trumpets did not melt into lumps of metal. . . .

As the year progressed however, new compositions became gradually less important to the Viennese and indeed to the Strauss brothers themselves. Theatre, as well as concert audiences steadily diminished, and eventually even an appearance of the "Waltz King" Johann could not guarantee the accustomed vast crowds of the summer concerts.

As war between Prussia and Austria became inevitable, the normally cosmopolitan Johann Strauss was converted to burning patriotism. He even suggested to the Emperor's adjutants that one of his and Jetty's houses in Vienna should be adapted as a hospital. The offer was actually taken up, but events developed so quickly that they simply overtook the Strauss brothers' efforts to contribute in their usual way. Josef's "Homage March", composed in honour of the Commander of the Northern Army, Benedek, was never performed! Johann announced a "Grand Corso Festival" in the Prater, originally scheduled for 17 June, postponed until the 24th, and again, by reason of continuing bad weather, to 1 July and now called "Victory Celebration". Rain and storms however enforced yet another adjournment until 8 July, but by that date Austria's defeat was conclusive and the proceeds from the eventual "Patriotic Festival" were once again devoted to the disabled soldiers.

In the autumn, the life of Vienna slowly resumed normality. During his involuntary leisure, Josef Strauss was inspired to sketch an enchanting tone-poem in polka-mazurka rhythm, which he presented in the Volksgarten on 21 October. It was "Die Libelle" (The Dragonfly). Later, Johann followed with the dreamy "Feenmärchen" (Fairy Tales) waltz, and the polka "Wildfeuer" (Wildfire). which title was derived from the season's programme of the Hofburgtheater. Josef appears to have rounded off the season with his waltz "Friedenspalmen" (Palms of Peace). Nobody could have foreseen what a superb harvest was yet to ripen from the impressions and inspirations of the year 1866.

The public were only aware that on New Year's Eve, in the significant gesture of his quick polka "Farewell", Josef dispatched the closing year with a parting kick!

VIII

Herbstrosen

p

Op. 232

To Johann and Josef Strauss it had been predictable for some time that the year 1867 would begin with a challenge for them. Johann was the first to be concerned. Vienna's male voice choir, the famous "Wiener Männergesang-Verein" decided, in view of the defeat by Prussia at Königgrätz, to abandon their customary "Fools' Evening" for the carnival of 1867, and replace it with a concert in which choral works could alternate with humorous items. They remembered that, in the summer of 1865, Johann Strauss had promised to dedicate a waltz to their society. The choir, at the instigation of its chorus-master Johann Herbeck, had at that time given a generally successful concert with the Strauss Orchestra in the "Neue Welt" but without Johann's promised composition; he had postponed work on the contribution because of his engagement in Pavlovsk. Eventually Josef had deputized for him and contributed, not specifically for the choir but for the concert series, a new polka, "Verliebte Augen" (Amorous Eyes).

The choir now energetically reminded Johann about "his" waltz and he rummaged through his sketches to find the draft of a composition for which he had in mind the title "An der schönen blauen Donau" (On the Beautiful Blue Danube). An elaborate tone-picture was planned for the introduction, in which the simple rising main waltz theme was also established and if one rightly interprets his hasty jottings, which are still in

Josef Strauss

existence, one can arrive at a conclusion that the extensive coda has been established right from the beginning. As the Männergesang-Verein required a concert waltz rather than a dance, the composer had to make some concessions. With his customary generosity, Johann immediately agreed to co-operate with them in the production of a work for men's voices; the waltz was eventually extended and the coda changed. On 22 January 1867, about three weeks before the carnival concert, the vocal parts of the "Blue Danube" were in print. As he later confided to Josef, Johann was "sorry about the beautiful coda", but a choral finale had, after all, its own requirements. At the first performance, the Wiener Männergesang-Verein under chorus-master Weinwurm, and accompanied by a regimental band, gave the waltz in its revised version. The Strauss Orchestra and the composer himself were playing before the Imperial Court and therefore not available! In its original form, the waltz was later presented in the Volksgarten.

In the 1867 carnival season, Josef Strauss was also faced with an almost insurmountable problem. It became his task to open the round of "representative balls", which this year fell rather flat in consequence of the "*hardly jocose mood*", as the *Wiener Zeitung* put it, with a dedication for the medical students. To top it all, the piece was to have the title "Delirien" (Deliriums)! What kind of a demand was this, to conjure up feverish dreams for the depressed mood of a public appearing in a half empty ballroom?

Josef Strauss saw this as a challenge. He illustrated the delirium in the fascinating sounds of the prelude: twenty-seven bars sufficed for a vision of tremendous forcefulness, and then, with an ingenious transition, the agitation of the feverish fantasy led into a spirited yet relaxed waltz. The principal melody of the work begins as in the "Transactionen", softly, and as it were above flowing ripples of sound. After a timorous rise it also seems to drop again, but in this waltz immediately rises, soaring higher and higher still up to a jubilant outbreak of the joy of living, unfolding spontaneously out of the delirium! Coincidentally, the "Delirien" and the "Blue Danube" (choral version) were entered next to each other in the publisher's ledger under the date, 22 January 1867. The two compositions are closely associated; they represent a part of the contest between the two brothers and if the one work is weighed against the other we can appreciate Johann's words, often repeated within the circle of his friends: "Pepi is the more gifted, I am merely the more popular. . . ."

The contrast between the essential characters of the brothers Johann and Josef was shown more particularly in two other compositions written for this carnival season. At the "Hesperus Ball", Johann performed his elegant and cultured waltz, "Künstlerleben" (Artist's Life); Josef followed him onto the rostrum, and replied with his waltz, written exactly a week earlier, "Marienklänge", named in honour of the Princess Marie von Kinsky. The elegiac motif of the opening has an insistent, almost strange air about it, (one columnist later wrote: "*one could happily die to this music*"), but the impetus of this lively waltz swept the dancers along with it. Likewise, everyone fell into a frenzy of delight, when Josef presented his actual ball dedication, the quick polka "Jocus" (Jocose)! It was un-doubtedly his second "Reisser" as, at the Concordia Ball, his polka "Allerlei" (Variety) had also been a smash-hit. The success was so great that Johann knew no peace until he scored an equalizer with the quick polka "Leichtes Blut" (High Spirits). The final "balance-sheet" read: six new pieces by Johann, eleven by Josef and eight by Eduard.

In the spring of 1867, Jetty and Johann entered upon the risky undertaking of presenting, at their own expense, a series of concerts in Paris in connection with the World Exhibition. As the Strauss Orchestra was committed to remaining in Vienna under the direction of his younger brothers, Johann entered into an arrangement with the Berlin musical director, Bilse. By virtue of his personality on the rostrum and the attraction of his compositions, Johann eventually overcame the extremely diffi-cult circumstances and finally achieved an overwhelming success. Right at the start, he was helped by the Princess Metternich who commissioned him to conduct for a Gala Ball given in the Austrian Embassy, attended by the French Royal couple and, indeed, "all Paris".

A little later, an Austrian military band, also in Paris, became winners of an international competition, and the attention of the Viennese was for weeks concentrated upon the French capital. Josef Strauss took this opportunity to slip quietly away for a rest-cure at Fusch in the Salzkammergut. At the beginning of August he had again suffered a collapse and, on 11 August 1867, he wrote from Salzburg:

> I arrived fairly well, but exhausted. I did not sleep all night in Linz. Whether this was due to excitement or reaction to events shortly before my departure, I do not know. I stayed in bed until 10 o'clock however, and then sat at the table where we were two years ago. I stayed there until half-past twelve, when I only had a little soup and then went into Salzburg, where I arrived at about half-past five, hungry, thirsty, very fatigued; I believe that the climate, the change of air, affect me this year more than they did two years ago because I am much weaker, in a much lower condition.

Never for a moment suspecting the nature of his ill-health, Josef was hoping for a quick recovery in the "genuine mountain air". As Eduard stated in his "Memoirs" (where, incidentally, he mistakenly placed this rest-cure in the year 1868), Josef was away "over a month; but, rather than finding the desired cure, he again fell deeply unconscious only two days after his return". Once more the diagnosis was "nervous fever" and again no serious investigation of the source of the trouble was undertaken.

At the closing concert of the season, Josef appeared "personally" at the head of the orchestra in the "Neue Welt" as though nothing had happened, and greeted the public with his new polka-mazurka, "In der Heimath" (In the Homeland). By this time at the latest, however, it must have been clear to Josef Strauss that his life was irrevocably approaching its end. In some compositions of this period we find melodies and harmonies which touch at emotions that were, for the time being at least, a closed book to his brother Johann who wished to remain, at any price, a man of "eternal youth". An awareness

of the inevitable departure seemed already to sound in the
"Marienklänge", and now this mood returned again in the first
great waltz of the new season. The title "Herbstrosen"
(Autumn Roses) appeared above the score, and perhaps simply
indicated that the composition was specifically written for the
first concert of the Strauss Orchestra's renewed association with
the "Floral Halls", but there may have been other conno-
tations. Shortly afterwards, Josef Strauss began to write his
dedication for the medical students' ball of 1868 – the
"Sphärenklänge" (Music of the Spheres). When this waltz was
first heard, on 21 January in the Sophiensaal, even the
superficial ball-reporters proved unusually observant: the *Fremdenblatt* reported, "It makes a strange impression to be musically
reminded of the next world at a medics' ball". Yet already in the
next sentence, the customary dull routine writing takes over:
"The festival progressed in the highest spirits . . ." Even later,
justice was rarely done to this waltz. After two years it was
associated in Vienna with sentimental legends, with superficial
enthusiasm about "a poetry which stirs you to tears", or it was
referred to as "a moving poem" and eventually a text was set to
it, strangely appearing as, "The spring is now awakened . . ."!
But this of all music needs no words, and no words can
interpret it.

It had of course to be recognized that such compositions were
not the ideal offering for a public which noisily sat down to eat
and drink in a Gasthaus garden, with music as background
entertainment. The Strauss concerts demanded a different
environment. It was fortuitous that, following his triumphs in
Paris, Johann Strauss travelled on to England and, in London,
came to know and appreciate the Promenade Concerts at
Covent Garden. In these cultured surroundings it was much
easier for him to be acknowledged than in the bustle of the Paris
performances. On his return to Vienna, Johann immediately
began to fashion his soirées "on the example of the English
Promenade Concerts".

On 19 January 1868, the first of these new style concerts was
held in the "Floral Halls". Around the orchestra was installed a

circle of seats for those who wanted to concentrate on the music while others, who only wished to hear a mere sprinkling of the sound, had the opportunity to promenade further back. The restaurant was banished to the ground floor, where a military band played the habitual "conversation music". The public welcomed the innovation; an important step had been made towards a closer connection between Viennese light music and symphonic music. It is significant of the conditions in Vienna during those years, that the initiative for this cultural development in the Viennese concert halls, extending over many decades, derives not from any "cultural institution" but from the Strauss Orchestra, founded specifically for the "waltz business".

For the first Promenade Concert, Johann contributed two new pieces, the Parisian "Figaro" polka and the polka-mazurka "Stadt und Land" (Town and Country), but took little part in providing works for the 1868 carnival. Only the "Concordia" Ball and the last "Bürgerball" (Citizens' Ball) in the Redouten-saal, were to receive dedications from his pen. As Josef caused another furore with a quick polka "Eingesendet" (Gone to Press), Johann was inspired to yet another competing piece – "Unter Donner und Blitz" (Under Thunder and Lightning). Josef was responsible for all the other carnival arrangements, but now, as Eduard did not want to be left out, this season's final figures showed: ten new works by Josef and seven by Eduard, as against only three by Johann Strauss.

In the spring also, Josef had to carry the main burden of the work, and this suited him well enough. He now became immersed in his activities, composing and arranging more ardently than ever, going to and fro between his study and the various concert venues. Later on, he even prided himself upon not having set foot in the Stephansplatz for a whole year. To combat the tremendous pressures, he played cards almost daily until the early hours of the morning, in the Hotel National or the coffee-houses of the Leopoldstadt. Occasionally he was invited by Johann and Jetty to their new home in Hietzing. Johann was also passionately fond of cards, but he practised his hobby with personal irony and playful humour. Josef on the other hand, as Jetty phrased it in a letter of 1868, ". . . sat as if at a funeral, and was always completely serious". On top of this, Josef smoked heavily, up to twenty cigars a day. He had obviously given himself up! In the spring of 1868, Johann Strauss had little time to worry about his brother. He worked, attentively shielded by Jetty, on his first operetta, "Die lustigen Weiber von Wien" (The Merry Wives of Vienna) which however was never fully completed, and is lost. Johann only appeared at the head of the orchestra to conduct his waltz "Geschichten aus dem Wienerwald" (Tales from the Vienna Woods) first at a fête for the Prince Hohenlohe, then at a concert in the Volksgarten and finally yet again at the summer concert of the Wiener Männergesang-Verein in the "Neue Welt". Josef supplemented the programme of the Volksgarten soirées with the first performance of three scenes from Wagner's opera *Die Meistersinger von Nürnberg* and two new pieces of his own composition: "Die Sirene" (The Siren) and "Eile mit Weile" (More Haste, less Speed). Josef had arranged his polka-mazurka "Dithyrambe" for the Männerges-ang-Verein, and had words written for it by Joseph Weyl, author of the text for the "Blue Danube". But Johann's "Sensationswalzer", as the press described his most famous waltz, ousted not only the "Dithyrambe" but also the "Meister-singer" from the centre of public interest. Johann had produced the appropriate companion piece to Josef's "Village Swallows".

The "Bundes-Schützenfest", a national shooting contest, now broke upon the Danube metropolis, but in all the attendant hubbub only two events stood out; the première of the immediately popular Josef Strauss waltz, "Wiener Fresken" (Viennese Frescoes) and the triumphant repeat of the "Blue Danube" at a "Monster Concert" in the Prater. Johann's "Hymn in three-quarter time" was virtually rediscovered, and acclaimed as the "Marseillaise of the Schützenfest".

On the other hand, a "musical joke" by Josef, which he introduced to the public at the "Neue Welt" was a complete flop. Spina hesitated over publishing this piece which was initially performed under the title of "Die Plaudertasche" (The Chatterbox). He eventually hid this genial sketch among other works in an album which was published in connection with the Schützenfest and, being convinced that the German visitors to the festival would not understand the very "Viennese" title, he substituted for "Plaudertasche" – "Plappermäulchen". Johann's "Perpetuum mobile" had thus found a counterpart that moreover, like Johann's virtuoso scherzo, was neither understood nor appreciated in Vienna for a long time.

Immediately following the turbulent close of the Schützenfest, it again became necessary to announce that Josef was "indisposed" as he was once more suffering from attacks of unconsciousness. Yet, arising out of this break-down, he found a new purpose in life: Johann made it clear to his brother that he definitely intended to concentrate on the composition of operettas, and that he had decided to take the opportunity to relinquish his titular office of Hofball-Musikdirektor. He hinted that the succession stood open for Josef and told him that he had already put forward tentative proposals in this direction. He had also learnt from Pavlovsk, that "Strauss & Co." were once more under consideration; Johann declared himself willing to recommend his brother there again.

These prospects awoke in Pepi, now a very sick man, an almost incomprehensible sense of well-being. Even the sudden death at Christmas of the publisher Carl Haslinger from a stroke, did not act as a warning to him. Josef appeared to set aside any thoughts of a similar fate. He suddenly viewed the future with optimism. He particularly looked forward at this time to his "competition" with Johann in the 1869 carnival; he had already prepared two particularly "Viennese" waltzes with which he was certain to have success. One was "Aquarellen" (Water Colours) and the other bore the title "Mein Lebenslauf ist Lieb' und Lust" (The Path of my Life is Joy and Pleasure).

Josef, as drawn by Johann.

Caroline, as drawn by Josef.

Die drei Sträusse.

"The three Strausses" (Josef Strauss and his brothers). A popular subject for the caricaturists since 1862, when the brothers made their first joint appearance. (From the short-lived journal *Rakettl*.)

(Above) The Strauss brothers – Eduard, Johann, Josef (a photo-montage); (below) Josef's orchestral transcription of Schumann's "Träumerei", one of the few remaining of over 500 such orchestrations.

73

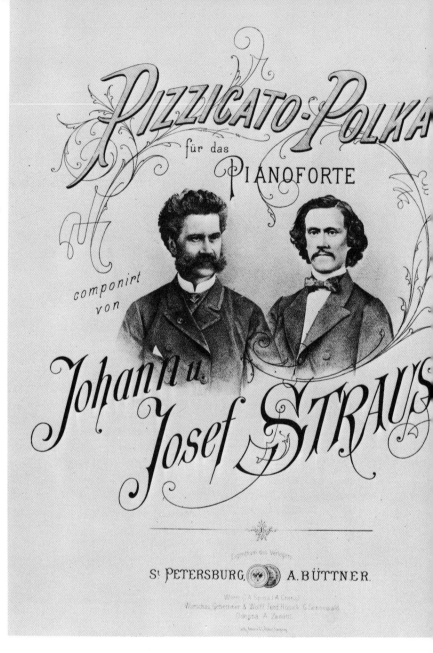

"Pizzicato–Polka", the joint masterpiece.

74

IX

Aus Der Ferne

pp dolcissimo   **Op. 270**

Josef Strauss threw himself wholeheartedly into his work for the lively carnival celebrations of 1869. Whereas, in the previous autumn, he had endeavoured to weigh seriousness against humour in a pensive waltz entitled "Ernst und Humor", he now turned solely to gaiety and the joy of living. Whenever he had the opportunity to determine the names of his new compositions, he constantly chose optimistic, charming and happy titles, for example: "Neckerei" (Teasing) for a mazurka, and "Frohsinn" (Good Humour) for a polka française. Two of his fastest and most dashing quick polkas celebrated the latest sports crazes, ice-skating and bicycling; – "Eislauf" and "Velocipede"! His waltzes no longer suggested melancholy and yearning but with short, pregnant melodies marked a return to "classical" Viennese dance music.

While Johann prepared to present his first truly choral waltz, "Wein, Weib und Gesang" (Wine, Woman and Song) at the "Fools' Evening" of the Männergesang-Verein on 2 February at the Dianasaal, Josef chose his most swinging and energetic dance for the "Hesperus Ball" of the Artists' Association on 1 February. Only in the quietly reflective Introduction did he seek to express the set title, "Aquarellen" (Water Colours). There followed an energetic "invitation to the dance", a sudden chord from the wind instruments, a tense pause – then the waltz burst forth with a "cut and thrust" characteristic known only in

75

Vienna; a challenging "what price the world" sound, that was never to be repeated except by the bold "Militärkapellmeister" Carl Michael Ziehrer in the maturity of his later years. The rhythm seemed to establish itself in opposition to the beat, and yet the melodies inexorably drew the dancers into the whirlpool on the floor of the "Dianabadsaal". As the waltz proceeded further, the more clearly was the brazen "hm-tata" of the long-since outmoded dances of fathers and forefathers uplifted by the soaring melodies; that sense of floating suspension was achieved which is, after all, the ideal of the genuine Viennese waltz.

"Wine, Woman and Song" is of course an ingenious composition, and it is clear why Richard Wagner preferred it, next to the "Blue Danube", above all other dances of Johann Strauss, whom he greatly admired. But "Aquarellen" is more elemental, and had greater vivacity. In this waltz, Josef Strauss had perhaps denied his own nature, yet had certainly surpassed himself. In his dedication for the Students' Ball on 7 February 1869 in the Redoutensaal, Josef once again achieved in the same season, a creation more boisterous, happier, more exuberant than that of his brother. A students' song ("Ich hab' den ganzen Vormittag") opened the introduction; another ("Mein Lebenslauf ist Lieb' und Lust"), crowned the coda and gave the work its title. In between however, Josef Strauss gave free rein to his temperament. The melody begins with an almost imperceptible hesitation, then wings its way in ever new, gently cradled rising motifs, skips along, sings, exults, and yes, the waltz even sobs! Fifty years of further development had been anticipated! The piece ends with happiness and high spirits. Johann was undeniably trumped and outbidden; he was not able to challenge his brother again before the following carnival season.

This time, in the incomplete carnival review, the count showed ten new pieces by Josef and five by Eduard; not before March did Johann Strauss introduce his three dedications together with two latecomers by his brothers. Intensive preparations for the season in Pavlovsk now began. Only a few comparatively minor matters had to be attended to beforehand.

Pepi paid a visit to the "Nasswalder" Association led by August Silberstein, and presented them with a Ländler (in polka-mazurka rhythm) in which, conscious of the style, he used a combination of two zithers, two violins, viola and cello. This little work ("Die Nasswalderin") remains a charming illustration of how supremely well Josef Strauss could express the spirit of folk music in his creations. Brother Johann's success was also not confined to the "Viennese" sphere; he triumphed later with the quick polka "Eljen a Magyar!" (Long Live the Magyars!) in Pest. Josef assisted on this occasion with his "Andrássy-Marsch".

Also in March, Vienna saw a celebration the like of which it had rarely experienced before. The factory owner Wertheim, organized (in the "Floral Halls") a festival for his workers, in connection with the completion of their 20,000th iron safe. As the *Vorstadt Zeitung* mockingly emphasized, "there sat the Countess, in elegant dress, next to the factory girl in linen frock, without the world coming to an end". Josef Strauss performed for this celebration, and transformed the company's widely known advertising slogan "Feuerfest!" (Fireproof!) into a jolly polka. In this work, the long forgotten sound of the smith's hammer echoes on down to our own day.

After a spectacular farewell-concert in the "Floral Halls", during the course of which both brothers honoured the King of Portugal, Johann with "Königslieder" (Songs for a King) and Josef with "Huldigungslieder" (Songs of Homage), they travelled together, with Jetty, via Warsaw to Pavlovsk. Immediately upon arrival they had problems. On 24 April, Jetty wrote to her sister-in-law Caroline, ". . . I had to organize everything in the rooms as well as in the kitchen, and we therefore had a great deal of work to do before we could procure a little comfort for ourselves."

On Easter Sunday, Pepi commented further in a letter to his wife:

. . . Of the rooms on the first floor, three have been taken away from us, but we have two on the ground floor instead. One is our drawing-room, and the other is Jetty's dressing- and sitting-room. Our bedrooms are on the first floor. My furnishings consist of a narrow wardrobe fitted with three shelves, and an impregnable three-drawer chest; you can imagine how my clothes are strewn about. My bed is very good, but my wash-stand is a rickety music-chest of Jean's turned upside down and covered with a linen cloth. The food is excellent, Jetty is invaluable, I have never eaten so well.

Josef also described his daily routine and from the many letters exchanged between Pavlovsk and Vienna, one can obtain an impression of the events which took place during that problematical summer. The misfortunes had in fact begun when, in making advance arrangements, Johann had overlooked the time difference between the Russian and the Western European calendars:

> I get up at nine o'clock and have breakfast – always alone, as Jean and Jetty sleep longer – at eleven o'clock I go to rehearsals which last until half-past one. I then work at my writing-desk on instrumentation and copying. Lunch is at about four o'clock, at half-past four a second rehearsal until six or half-past. I then go home, tired, and work again on the repertoire. We have our evening meal at about ten o'clock and then we chat . . . Jean has suffered a grievous loss through his error with the dates. The musicians all arrived fourteen days early and he had to compensate them, thereby sacrificing 700 roubles – he also had to buy each little instrument, which accounted for another 1,700 roubles. I shall have done very well if I manage to retain 1,000 roubles out of my fee of 3,000 . . .

A profit was thus hardly possible. For the moment however, Josef's confidence remained unshaken, and on 19 April he assured his wife:

> I have to put up with many disagreeable things, but I accept them all, just to make possible a happy and carefree life for you. I work for you, for the sacrifice you have made by living in such poor surroundings these twelve years.

The question soon arose, whether the main object of the undertaking, which was to establish Josef in Pavlovsk for several years, was possible to achieve. The directors appeared to be non-committal. Josef was nevertheless able to report on the success of his personal début which took place on 14 May:

Jean was received like an old favourite. He could not begin to play before taking many bows. I had to appear only in the last part. Jean introduced me, and I received a rather enthusiastic reception. I had to bow many times, and a minute passed before I could raise the baton to play the "Lockpolka" (Enticement Polka), which after two recalls I had to repeat. Similarly, the following pieces were also received with the greatest applause.

In Pavlovsk, Josef was full of a yearning for his wife; it was expressed in each of his letters. He composed the polka-mazurka "Aus der Ferne" (From Afar): once again a pastel painting was created with delicate lines and unusual tone-colours. Josef was by this time convinced that he would receive a further engagement in Russia for the following year, and looked forward to walking with his wife in the magnificent park of Pavlovsk – ". . . would that we had such a park in Vienna!". On his wedding anniversary he wrote home:

Immer mit Dir
nur durch Dich und
ewig für Dich!

(Always with you
only because of you and
eternally for you!)

In this relaxed mood, Johann had an idea:

I advised my brother to compose something which would really catch the imagination in Petersburg, and suggested to him, a pizzicato polka. He was not very keen on the idea – he was always indecisive – eventually I proposed that we two should produce the polka as a joint effort. He took up the idea. . . ."

Jetty, who knew of this plan, still showed herself to be somewhat sceptical in her letter to Caroline on 13 June: "Pepi and Jean are now writing a polka together – this will be something new. . . ."

The "Pizzicato-Polka" however, is the finest proof of the brotherly co-operation eventually achieved between Johann and Josef Strauss. Immediately, from its "trial-run" on 24 June, and then again at the official première at a benefit concert on 6 July (together with Johann's "Egyptian March") the piece was a resounding success.

Despite the undoubted success with the public at Pavlovsk, the atmosphere in the "Vauxhall" gradually deteriorated to the point where Johann was in a state of noisy agitation and working in that situation got on Josef's nerves. On 26 June he confided to Caroline:

> I do not like the engagement. It is a continuous struggle to shake the public out of their blasé attitude. But, if I am offered favourable terms, I will accept for two years (I confess to you – you my only and dearest possession) so as to leave you a modest fortune. That is my wish!

Josef Strauss constantly considered his prospects for the future. In the letter of 26 June he remarks in closing: "As I don't want to practise the trade of a beer-fiddler, I am turning to

Notes made by musicians F. A. Zimmermann, a member for many years of the Strauss Orchestra in Pavlovsk, who kept detailed records: the strokes indicate "recalls" by the audience, and the circles indicate repeat performances.

other kinds of composition". From Vienna however, there now
came alarming news that provoked his anger. On 6 July, Josef
gave vent to his grievance:

> Dearest, only wife – do not be too upset at the latest news that you learn
> from this letter. We have received the information, that Eduard is setting
> himself up independently, and this must be prevented. If Mama supports
> this undertaking of Eduard's, our co-operation will be at an end. The
> orchestra will be re-organized from the excellent talent available locally
> and will proceed to operate under its own steam. I long for my
> independence, it is high time also, to give you a new status. I wrote to
> Mama yesterday, that my complete submission in the Hirschenhaus
> already disgusts me, that my accommodation no longer suffices, that I
> want to establish myself in a different situation. Dearest wife, help me –
> do not be influenced by consideration for the others, the freedom that
> you have wanted for so long will come. Just be shrewd, dear little
> wife. . . .

In the meantime, Jetty had learned that her brother-in-law
stood little chance of continuing his activities in Pavlovsk the
following year. In a letter to Gustav Lewy she appended the
remark, "I understand it too, now that I know him better". But
then again it was Jetty herself, who in a detailed letter of 26
August to Caroline was again hopeful:

> Business is going well and the outlook is not at all bad – if only Pepi
> possessed some of Jean's gift of talking to people he would be sitting
> pretty; but he is too timid, reserved, too little a man of the world, and
> that comes from his stay-at-home tendency. An artist must not hide his
> light under a bushel, his creations on their own are not enough – he must
> stand up for them himself. Pepi is a complete introvert and scorns all
> outward appearance – but today's world sets great store by appearances!

Johann's frame of mind improved again as the summer drew to
its close. At the second benefit concert on 6 September 1869, he
had produced a new "hit": the polka "Im Pawlowsk-Walde",
which was later to be introduced in Vienna under the title "Im
Krapfenwaldl".*

This time, Josef was unable to register a parallel success. On
10 September he wrote to his wife:

---

*The title denotes a change of venue to a popular spot in the Vienna Woods
on the edge of the city. (P. G. P.)

I don't look at all well. I have become paler, my cheeks more hollow, I am losing my hair, I am on the whole very run down. I have no incentive to work; one's whole imagination is stifled here by sheer boredom and eternal monotony. The uncertainty in which I live, not knowing whether I shall be engaged or not, makes me all the more ill and dissatisfied. . . . Had I foreseen all this: that we literally would all be living together, that my business would be providing not only for me but for everybody, that Eduard would be so awkward, etc. – all things considered, I would have made myself free and independent before now.

On 17 September, mother Anna energetically intervened in the affair; vexed about Josef's letter of 6 July, she again went into the attack against him:

Eduard will not go under; I and my two daughters will also manage to live – better a parting of the ways than such a miserable existence. I do not sleep, cannot eat, there is no rest, nothing but guile, strife, grudges between you – I don't want to know any more. You are concerned about nothing but your own families, and we are the "poor relations". Thank you very much! May God one day forgive you for it. I have not deserved it – this ingratitude.

In the meantime, the intentions of the directors had become clear – they were to give no further consideration to Josef's future. Josef filled with renewed energy, reacted promptly and decided: "This more than suits me. Bilse has been engaged here and it is my intention to succeed him in his former post. I have therefore to make my arrangements for Warsaw."

Thus he wrote to Caroline on 27 September and requested her to make his resolve known publicly in Vienna. Josef was again as optimistic as he had been at the beginning of the year and wrote, in addition to the "En passant" polka, a waltz, "Frohes Leben" (A Happy Life) and finally also the quick polka "Ohne Sorgen!" (Without a Care).

On 14 November, Josef appeared together with Johann before the Viennese public with the last of the Pavlovsk compositions, and the "Pizzicato Polka". With both the "Floral Halls" and the Volksgarten for the time being lost because of disagreements, the orchestra began the autumn season in the "Sophiensaal". Now however, Johann concluded an agreement with the Gesellschaft der Musikfreunde for "Strauss Concerts" to be held on Sundays as soon as their new concert hall was opened on the bank of the Wien river (now Karlsplatz). This compensated for all the losses.

Under the watchful eye of their mother, Josef and Eduard Strauss concluded a new contract which stipulated down to the smallest detail, the future terms and conditions of their co-operation. Everything thus appeared to be in good order again. If nobody else, however, Jetty at least had a presentiment that catastrophe within the family was imminent.

X

Hesperus-Bahnen

In the autumn of 1869, unperturbed and at a dashing pace which
until then his cautious, timid nature had rarely permitted, Josef
Strauss forged ahead with the plans that he had made in
Pavlovsk. On 10 October he received the final decision of the
railway company, that the German conductor Bilse was to be
engaged for the 1870 season in his place. At 2.00 a.m. on 11
October he informed his wife of this and on 15 October he
arrived in Warsaw to look over the "Schweizerthal" establishment where Bilse had enjoyed a profitable season the previous
summer. Still furious about Eduard's intention to go on tour,
Josef hastily concluded a contract with the proprietor for the
1870 summer season. From 15 May to 15 September, he was to
lease the establishment on payment of a fixed sum, with the
right to present concerts and entertainments under his own
management. The agreement was anything but favourable, but
Josef concealed the truth and let it be thought in Vienna that he
had been "engaged on the most favourable terms".

At home, Josef found everyone against him. The neutral
refuge of the "Sophiensaal", no doubt about it, served as an
emergency solution to enable him to begin the winter concerts.
Apart from this hall, only the "Kursalon" in the Stadtpark
remained at the orchestra's disposal – a venue not yet fully
established at that time, and attracting far fewer patrons than
did the Volksgarten. Josef persisted however in his antipathy

towards Herr von Szabó, the lessee of the Volksgarten Café, and obstinately insisted on giving his concerts in the "Kursalon". Johann in the meantime had begun to forge new links with Szabó who, although it could not be foreseen at that time, was shortly to announce a new series of "popular concerts" by the Strauss Orchestra.

Josef reacted with a vehemence that threw his mother into a state of panic. All at once she realized the situation – for which she herself was largely to blame – and turned despairingly to Jetty!

I make so bold as to beg of you to exert all appropriate influence on Jean, not to reproach Pepi with regard to the Szabó soirées. Josef cannot talk with Szabó, and has this trouble with his head. It is my opinion that Josef should be protected and released from the Warsaw commitment. His health will not stand it, seeing to everything himself, unless Jean were to go with him. (We must) allow Eduard to dabble alone until Josef regains his health, otherwise he is lost. The attack that he (Josef) had yesterday evening was, he said, like a stroke, and this must not happen again. Lina is heartless, she has no idea of the weakness in his head, it is a misfortune for him to have such a wife; I wish that I could speak to you alone concerning the journey, his condition is dangerous. . . .

Whatever Jetty may have undertaken to do about this letter from her mother-in-law, she did in fact achieve nothing. Only the start of the carnival season succeeded in pouring oil on the troubled waters. At this time, interest was centred upon the opening of the Musikverein building. The final stone was laid on 5 January, the first concert took place the following day and, on 15 January, the first ball was held in the great gilded hall. Naturally, all three brothers were present and played their dedications: Johann, the waltz "Freut euch des Lebens" (Enjoy Life), Josef, the polka "Künstlergruss" (Artist's Greeting) and Eduard, the mazurka "Eisblume" (Frost Flower). From then on, the carnival programme drew to a close without further rancour. Josef's compositions, including the waltzes "Frauenwürde" (Women's Virtue), "Nilfluthen" (Waters of the Nile), "Tanzprioritäten" (Dance Priorities) and "Rudolphsklänge" (named after the Crown Prince), exhibited without exception the unbroken force of his inspiration. For the final production,

Josef announced even more outstanding works: the polka-mazurka "Die Emanzipierte" (The Emancipated), clearly an allusion to his wife Caroline, and the quick polka, "Jockey". One waltz was yet to follow, the ball for which it was intended having been postponed – the "Hesperus-Bahnen" (Orbit of the Evening Star). The composer had time to mould this piece painstakingly beyond the limitations of routine work, and gave it "the charm of his own personal stamp".

On 23 February, before the close of the carnival season, Anna Strauss died in her 69th year. Josef collapsed unconscious on his mother's death-bed, and recovered only after extensive efforts by the doctor. Johann did not come near the house, nor did he attend the funeral.

With the death of his mother, who had to the last opposed his plans (and in so doing, eventually gained the support of Caroline), Josef felt more than ever the necessity of going his own way. In Pavlovsk he had recognized, clearly and undeniably, that he must achieve independence and that he must relinquish the laborious duties in Vienna if he was ever to create the works that he felt himself destined to write. Who would have thought then, that in his artistic imagination he had long since overcome frontiers which Johann, with all the genius of his carefree creations, had not yet even perceived? And still he had so many ideas, plans, dreams. He must therefore try his luck, at any price! Nobody was able to succeed in changing his mind!

On 13 March 1870, Johann, Josef and Eduard appeared together on the rostrum of the Musikverein for the first time, to direct the traditional "Carnevalsrevue". True, some voices were raised in protest against the alleged "desecration of the house" with dance music, but they were soon silenced by the overwhelming majority of the Viennese. At the very first Strauss Concert, the hall was filled to overflowing and hundreds had to be turned away. Also in the Musikverein, on 4 April, the previously postponed ball of the "Hesperus" Association took place, and Josef performed the waltz ("Hesperus-Bahnen") that proved to be his last. Again, a gently insinuating melody rose in a dreamlike flight of fancy, again the form was expanded, and yet again were "not only the feet inspired to dance, but the emotions aroused".

On Easter Sunday, 17 April, Josef Strauss conducted in the Musikverein, his last concert in Vienna. He took his departure with the polka, "Heiterer Muth" (Cheerful Courage). On the Tuesday, the press had this to say: "Herr Strauss enjoyed and received from the public the greatest distinction and honour, in view of which he may with little doubt feel assured that upon his return he will be equally well received."

On 25 April, accompanied by the already very sick "Aunt Pepi", Josef Strauss travelled to Warsaw. On the very day after their arrival, there began a chain of disasters. Music and instruments, not to mention personal effects, were held up at Customs due to incorrect declaration of the luggage. They were unable to move into the promised lodgings. Above all, the orchestra, comprising musicians from various countries was incomplete! Only after Josef's desperate call to Eduard for help, was the personnel supplemented. Even so, it was not possible to keep the scheduled opening date for the season, 15 May. Josef lacked not only Johann's rhetoric, but his talent for organization. On 17 May he wrote: "Dear Jean, I am disconsolate. No prospect of a beginning. By the time that this letter is in your hands the catastrophe will have reached its highest peak".

After a delay of one week the concerts in the "Schweizerthal" were able to begin. "My first appearance was favourable" reported Josef to his wife. The undertaking appeared to consolidate but on 1 June, Josef collapsed at the conductor's rostrum and had to be carried unconscious to his apartment. The doctors confirmed a cerebral attack.

Caroline was immediately advised, and on 5 June she travelled to Warsaw. There was little that she could do to help her husband; he was partly paralysed and much of the time unconscious. The family's worries were now to a great extent concerned with the business. In all haste, Musikdirektor Carlberg, who had lamentably failed with his "Symphony

Orchestra", was rushed off to Poland to substitute "provision-ally" for the sick Josef Strauss. On 15 June a further attack ended all hope of Josef's recovery. There immediately spread, not only in Vienna, but all over Europe, the rumour that he had been beaten up by some drunken Russians. In vain the family denied it; the official denial was not believed.

Jetty and Johann eventually joined Josef in Warsaw on 27 June. The nervous Johann, however, became so agitated on the journey that upon their arrival Jetty first required attention for him! On returning to Vienna, Johann described his brother's illness as "typhoidal head complaint, brought upon him by excessive strain".

On 17 July it proved possible for Josef to be brought back to Vienna. From time to time he was fully conscious, but there was nothing more that could be done for him at home. Josef Strauss died on 22 July 1870 at half-past one in the afternoon, in his 43rd year. The cause of death was presumed to be the bursting of a tumour on the brain. Caroline strictly withheld permission for an autopsy, and consequently no precise diagnosis could be established.

Josef had placed himself at his family's disposal because they needed him. Thus it became his destiny to be part of this family and eventually to be absorbed into the superficial, trivial concept: "Heut spielt der Strauss!" ("Strauss plays today!") But he was an independent character, a genius of a special order. Johann was right, for all musicians Josef is the more interesting Strauss even though "der Schani", the "Waltz King", was always the more popular.

Mother Anna Strauss, in 1869.

(Above) The "Schweizerthal" in Warsaw; (below) Eduard's report on his brother's illness. Josef died before the letter reached the recipient.

Karoline, with her father's portrait.

Strauss concerts in the Musikverein: (above) Eduard I continued until 1901 with the concerts founded by Josef and himself in 1870; (below) his grandson, Eduard II, conducting on 4 March 1954, to commemorate the 150th anniversary of the birth of Father Strauss.

94

XI

Extempore

J. Strauss: op. 25 Kadi-Qua.

Strauss-Reiterer: Cake-Walk.

Concerning the posthumous fame of Josef Strauss – "Musik-direktor und Compositeur" – and his legacy, several things are worthy of note. Only a day after his decease, the official records subsequently giving the nature of his death as "Blutzersetzung" (decomposition of the blood), everybody was saying that Pepi might have protected himself more than he did. In the *Neue Wiener Tagblatt*, in the *Wanderer*, the *Presse*, the *Fremdenblatt* and the *Morgenpost*, it was asserted that from early youth Josef had been sick, and that he should be seen as a sacrifice to his profession.

The *Morgenpost* commented appropriately: "Everyone who knew him will surely shed a tear for him: he was not only an artist, but also a man of honour and spirit." The *Neue Wiener Tagblatt* published a column saying among other things:

Josef – with your uniquely personal and winning dual personality, so boldly stylish, so spiritedly Viennese, so light-hearted among your circle of friends – and yet so full of artistic vision when in the company of your own muse, only spurring others on to such high spirits through your seemingly gentle baton.

Finally, the *Morgenpost* returned again to Josef's fate, and wrote:

A good spirit of the Viennese scene has departed. We have all suffered a loss in that we shall never again look at that handsome, clever, coquettishly pale countenance. Dead! And he died before he could realize the most precious ambition of his life – the composition of a grand opera.

The family also expected to come across a work for the theatre among Josef's effects. His daughter Karoline (married name Aigner) wrote on a number of occasions after 1910, maintaining that on the death of her father there must have been several packages of music, including a stage-work expressly given to her mother to enable her to raise money "in case of need"! In this connection, Lina in fact spoke of an operetta! Eduard Strauss repeatedly denied this statement and also contested it in his "Memoirs". It is certainly beyond dispute that Josef's estate passed initially into Johann's custody. It was in his hands until after Jetty's sudden death in April 1878, when he left the Hietzing palace in great haste. Not until then did Eduard – so at least he constantly stated – take over Josef's effects. There was however, only one bundle of compositions – music that was already in print. Eduard asked his brother whether that was all there was. He knew full well that Josef had written various other melodies "suitable for an opera", also choral works such as "An die Nacht" (To the Night) and "Wagnerklänge". Johann replied that *he* had no recollection of any other package.

Since that time it has constantly been asserted in articles and even in some books, that melodies originating from material left behind by Josef were used by Johann in some of his operettas – in *Die Fledermaus* for example. Certainly no proof to support this contention has ever been produced. It is certain though, that throughout his life Josef never objected to deputizing occasionally for his brother as a composer.

Eduard himself destroyed a whole series of his brother's works, together with almost all pot-pourris and arrangements from the archives of the Strauss Orchestra, which Josef had laboured strenuously to produce, (more than 500 pieces, including the *Tristan* and *Meistersinger* arrangements). How this came about is revealed in a report by a manufacturer of ovens, published later in the *Neue Wiener Journal*:

> The archives of the Herr Hofball-Musikdirektor Eduard Strauss went up in flames at my factory. On 22 October 1907, there arrived first a vehicle-load of heavy parcels of sheet music. In the afternoon, before two o'clock, Eduard Strauss appeared in my office with his manservant. I tried to talk him into abandoning the idea. Strauss stared straight in front of him for a while, then he cried out "I cannot!" With that we went into the factory where there were two large kilns for the firing of tiles and pottery. Eduard seated himself in an armchair in front of one of the kilns. My workmen opened the parcels and in front of the Herr Hofball-Musikdirektor's eyes, scattered the sheets of music into the consuming flames of the huge fire-box. Strauss was visibly moved as he caught sight of certain pieces which held special memories of his family. He stood up, looked away, or went back into the office for a while. He did not leave the factory however until the last sheet of music was burned. One can perhaps visualize the extent of the archives when I say that the burning of the material, which included original manuscripts and unpublished works, took from two o'clock in the afternoon until seven in the evening.

To this report need only be added that a catalogue of the Strauss Archives that Eduard himself had printed after his retirement from leading the orchestra in 1901 still included, for example, his brother's interesting concert waltz "Ideale" and the "Klänge aus der Ober- und Unterwelt". It is probable that the Romance "An die Hoffnung" (To Hope), played at the memorial concert for Josef given in the Musikverein in the autumn of 1870, and appreciatively spoken of by Johann Strauss in his last years, also fell victim to the flames.

The adventure of the Warsaw concerts of 1870 was a disaster. Josef's sister Netti, who was dispatched to Warsaw to relieve the desperately ill Aunt Pepi (Josephine Waber, née Streim, died on 21 November 1870) was obliged to make constant demands for subsistence from Vienna, in order to meet her expenses. It was not until Philipp Fahrbach was sent (much too late) to Poland, that some success was eventually assured.

In accordance with the terms of the business contract drawn up in 1869, Eduard looked after the interests of his brother's widow. In this he acted correctly, but by no means magnanimously. Caroline Strauss died on 22 November 1900 in Hainfeld, Lower Austria, in the most modest circumstances.

In the years following Josef's death, the significance of the Strauss Orchestra on the Vienna scene steadily declined. Eduard was certainly not to blame for this; for thirty years he maintained with distinction not only his position at the head of the orchestra, but also his office as Hofball-Musikdirektor. Vienna's society had changed however. The substitution of the former "Citizens' Balls" by celebrations of the "Industrial Societies" was but one of many signs of the times. In the broad area of open air concerts, "conversation-music" and soon also in the ballrooms, it was the military bands that were to take over. At the same time there developed a vogue for the folk-singers of various kinds, and finally, typical of Vienna, the unique "Schrammel" ensemble.

The Strauss Orchestra, with its ambitious programmes in which the Viennese dance constantly vied with operatic and symphonic works, and where even organ improvisations by Anton Bruckner did not seem out of place, gradually found itself confined to the Sunday concerts in the Musikverein. From 1878 onwards, "der schöne Edi" undertook annual concert tours in order to survive.

Josef's name was gradually forgotten, his works being attributed simply to "Strauss". Not until after Johann's death and the surprising success of the operetta *Wiener Blut*, which made use of his dance themes, were Josef's compositions again remembered. Ernst Reiterer utilized them in the operetta *Frühlingsluft*, and because of the success of this piece, the recipe was repeated several times over: "Take a waltz and make a song of it, take a polka for a duet, and a quadrille for example, for a cakewalk!"

But this had nothing to do with Josef Strauss. . . .

Appendix 1

The Most Important Strauss Venues

(Abbreviations in parentheses are referred to in the catalogue of works.)

Bierhalle, 15th district, Mariahilferstrasse, (BH): début of Lanner's son in 1853. Josef Strauss conducted at certain festivals up to 1856.

Blumensaele der Gartenbaugesellschaft, (Floral Halls), 1st district, Parkring (FH): concert-hall and ballroom from 26.12.1864. Josef conducted at the opening, and between October 1867 and March 1869, and on special occasions.

Dianabadsaal, 2nd district, Obere Donaustrasse, (DS): concert-hall and ballroom from 12.11.1860. Josef conducted up to 1862 (début of Eduard). 1863, début of C. M. Ziehrer. Mostly special balls. Wiener Männergesang-Verein concert with première of the "Blue Danube" in 1867.

Dommayers Casino, 13th district, Hietzinger Hauptstrasse, (Dom): established 1787. Johann (son) début, 1844. Josef conducted concerts and festivals up to 1870.

Musikverein, 1st district, Karlsplatz, (MV): Strauss Concerts from 1870.

Neue Welt, Hietzing, (NW): Strauss concerts from opening, 1861.

Pavlovsk, (30 km from St. Petersburg) railway terminus (Vauxhall) (Pav): concert and dance hall from 1838. Josef conducted in 1862 and 1869.

Redoutensaal in der Hofburg, 1st district, Josephsplatz, (Red): made available for special concerts and balls.

Schwenders Etablissement, 15th district, Schwenderplatz, (Schw): developed from modest origins to become Vienna's largest place of entertainment – the Colosseum from January 1865. Regular balls and special festivals.

Sofien(bad)saal, 3rd district, Marxergasse (SBS): concert and dance hall from 1846, opening conducted by Strauss (father), since when, uninterrupted balls and festivals: Josef until 1870, and thereafter Eduard.

Sperl, 2nd district, Kleine Sperlgasse, (Sp): dance hall since 1807. Strauss (father) director of music from 1829. Josef's début, 1853. Concerts and balls with brief interruptions until 1867.

Ungers Casino, Hernals, (site is now metro station Alserstrasse) (U): was Vienna's largest "Kaffeehausgarten". Strauss (father), Fahrbach, Johann Strauss (son). Josef's début as composer, 1853. Sold and made smaller in 1864, demolished in 1895.

K.K. Volksgarten, 1st district, Ringstrasse (VG): opened in 1823 with coffee-house (and adjacent "Garden of Paradise"). Concerts and soirées since opening. Strauss (father), Lanner and Fahrbach; from 1849, Johann Strauss (son); Josef, with interruptions until 1869.

Weghubers Caféhaus, 1st district, Museumstrasse, (Weg): enlarged, with garden, in 1861. Josef conducted up to 1862. Bankruptcy in 1865.

Grosser Zeisig, 7th district, Burggasse 2, (GZ): Strauss (father); Johann and Josef, up to 1869.

Appendix 2

Catalogue of Works

W = waltz, Wil = waltz in Ländler style, L = Ländler (country dance), P = polka, Pf = Polka française (French polka), PM = polka-mazurka, Ps = Schnell (quick) polka, Potp = Potpourri, Qu = Quadrille.

Op. No.	Title and Dedication	First performance date/venue	
–	Abendläuten, Idylle (Appeared only in Russia)	13.9.62	Pav
160	Abend-Stern, Pf (The artists' association, "Hesperus")	3.2.64	DS
174	Actionen, W. (For the Lawyers' Ball)	31.1.65	SBS
76	Adamira-Polka	1.60	
–	Allegro fantastique (Unprinted, lost)	28.8.62	Pav
219	Allerlei, Ps (The Authors and Journalists Association "Concordia")	12.2.67	SBS

72	Amanda, PM	1.60	
119	Amaranth, Pf	3.3.62	DS
49	Die Amazone, PM	3.60	
118	Amazonen-Quadrille	18.1.62	DS
147	Amouretten, Pf	27.6.63	NW

–	An die Hoffnung, Romanze	13.9.65	Pav
	(Unprinted, lost)		
–	An die Nacht, Ode für Männerchor und	17.10.58	VG
	Orchester (Lost)		
123	Angelica, Pf	29.5.62	NW
268	Andrássy-Marsch	16.3.69	Pest
	(Performed at a "Festival of		
	Remembrance")		
258	Aquarellen, W	1.2.69	DS
	(The artists' association, "Hesperus")		

167	Arabella-Polka	2.8.64	NW
24	K. K. Österreichischer Armee-Marsch	18.8.56	VG
	(. . . Archduke Wilhelm)		
215	Arm in Arm, PM	16.2.67	SBS

143	Associationen, W	21.1.63	Red
	(The Association of Industrial Societies)		
270	Aus der Ferne, PM	22.6.69	VG
14	Avantgarde-Marsch	23.4.56	GZ
8	Bacchanten-Quadrille	56	
30	Ball-Silhouetten, W	21.1.57	Sp
10	Bauern-PM	56	
94	Bellona, PM ("The Goddess of War")	2.10.60	VG

199	Benedek-Marsch (1866)		
58	Bivouac (= Biwak)-Quadrille	6.7.58	VG
206	„Blaubart"-Qu (J. Offenbach)	9.66	
106	Blitz-Polka	12.5.61	
	(For a fireworks festival in the Prater Park)		
55	Bon-Bon, P	6.6.58	U
188	Bouquet-Ps	26.12.64	FH
	(Opening of the "Floral Halls")		
129	Brennende Liebe, PM	9.11.62	Sp
252	Buchstaben, Pf	10.7.68	VG
–	Bundes-Armee-Marsch	7.6.57	
	(For a festival on the "Glacis", identical with Op. 24?)		
145	Cabriole-Ps	3.8.63	NW
–	Cap(p)rice für Klavier (Autograph, unprinted)		
65	Caprice-Quadrille	59	
–	Caroussel-Quadrille	6.10.60	U
	(Unprinted, lost)		
200	Carriere-Ps	22.6.66	VG
180	Causerie-Polka	5.2.65	Sp
42	La Chevaleresque, PM	57	
156	Die Clienten, W	2.2.64	SBS
175	Colosseum-Quadrille	8.1.65	Schw
	(For the opening of Schwender's "Colosseum")		
176	Combinationen, W	14.2.65	DS
	(For the students of technology)		
–	Concertmarsch	11.9.53	U
	(Unprinted, lost)		
257	Concordia! Pf	26.1.69	SBS
	(The Authors and Journalists Association, "Concordia")		

Trio

260	Consortien, W	31.1.69	Red
	(The Industrial Societies)		
224	„Crispino"-Qua (Ricci)	17.5.67	VG
37	Csikós-Quadrille	57	
81	Cupido, Pf	2.60	

84	Cyclopen-Polka	20.2.60	SBS
97	Débardeurs-Quadrille	26.1.61	DS
53	Defilir-Marsch	6.6.58	U
212	Delirien, W	22.1.67	SBS
	(The medical students)		

191	Deutsche Grüße, W	28.1.66	Red
	(Pauline Fürstin Metternich-Winneburg)		

146	Deutscher Union-Marsch	17.8.63	VG
149	Deutsche Sympathien, W	17.8.63	VG
	(Both for the "Battle of Leipzig Festival")		
95	Diana-Pf	12.11.60	DS
	(Opening of the Dianabad Hall)		
32	Dioscuren-Quadrille	16.2.57	SBS
243	Disputationen, W	18.2.68	Red
	(The students of Vienna)		
236	Dithyrambe, PM	13.2.68	FH
	Dithyrambe (Version for male voices)	22.6.68	NW
164	Dorfschwalben aus Österreich, W	6.9.64	VG
	(The author of the novel of the same name, Dr. August Silberstein)		

107	Dornbacher Rendez-vous-Polka	17.6.61	
	(Opening of the restaurant of that name)		
173	Dynamiden (Geheime Anzeihungskräfte), W	30.1.65	Red
	(The Industrial Societies)		

–	Ebbe und Fluth, Phantasiestücke (Unprinted, lost)		
148	Edelweiß, PM	3.10.63	Sp
247	Eile mit Weile, Ps	19.6.68	VG
240	Eingesendet! Ps (The Authors and Journalists Association, "Concordia")	4.2.68	SBS

171	Einzugs-Marsch (The return of Austrian troops from Schleswig-Holstein)	6.12.64	VG
261	Eislauf, Ps	2.69	
74	Elfen-Polka	25.7.59	U
282	Die Emanzipierte, PM	17.2.70	FH

273	En passant, Pf	5.10.69	Pav
254	Ernst und Humor, W	11.10.68	FH
12	Die Ersten nach den Letzten, W	7.54	U

1	Die Ersten und Letzten, W	28.8.53	U
86	Erzherzog Carlmarsch (In connection with the unveiling of the monument to Archduke Carl, in "Hero's Square")	25.5.60	VG
208	Etiquette-Pf	18.11.66	VG
82	Euterpe, PM	2.60	VG
194	Expensnoten, W (= Expensen) (The law students)	23.1.66	SBS

115	Folichon-Qu, nach beliebten Motiven	14.1.62	DS
193	For ever! Ps	29.1.66	SBS
103	Fortunio-Magellone-Daphnis-Qu	14.5.61	GZ
	(On themes by Offenbach)		
–	La forza del Destino, Potp (Verdi)	7.5.65	VG
	(Unprinted, lost)		
–	La Francaise, P	2.7.54	U
	(Unprinted, lost)		
47	Frauenblätter, W	2.58	
166	Frauenherz, PM	6.9.64	VG

277	Frauenwürde, W	30.1.70	Red
	(The Lawyers' Ball committee)		
253	Freigeister, Ps	15.9.68	VG
128	Freudengruße, W	9.11.62	Sp

207	Friedenspalmen, W	8.66	VG
177	Frisch auf! PM	9.2.65	SBS
272	Frohes Leben, W	6.9.69	Pav
264	Frohsinn, Pf	27.1.69	FH
44	Fünf Kleebladl'n, WiL	31.8.57	U

159	Gablenz-Marsch	28.3.64	VG
	(In honour of the brave Field Marshal)		
251	Die Galante, P	18.7.68	FH
237	Gallopin-Ps	13.2.68	FH

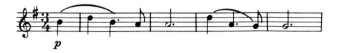

232	Herbstrosen, W	13.10.67	FH
157	Herold-Quadrille	25.1.64	SBS
31	Herzbleamerln, PM im Ländlerstyle	2.57	

172	Herztöne, W	17.1.65	SBS

279	Hesperusbahnen, W	4.4.70	MV
	(The artists' association "Hesperus")		
116	Hesperus-Ball-Tänze, W	26.2.62	DS
	(The artists' association "Hesperus")		
220	Hesperus-Ländler	27.1.67	FH
	(Dedicated to "Hesperus" and performed at the association's "Peasant Evening")		
–	Hinter den Coulissen, Qu	28.2.59	SBS
	(In collaboration with Johann Strauss)		
242	Hochzeitsklänge, W	1.3.68	FH
	(The King of Hanover)		
255	Huldigungslieder, W	4.4.69	FH
	(For the birthday celebrations of the King of Portugal)		
–	Österreichischer Huldigungsmarsch	15.3.57	VG
	(For the happy return of the royal couple from Italy) (Unprinted, lost)		
–	Hyazinth-Polka	19.3.62	Schw
–	Ideale, Concertwalzer	15.6.58	VG
	(Both unprinted, lost)		
163	Idylle, PM	15.7.64	VG
88	Immergrün, PM	19.6.60	VG
–	Impromptu (Andante) für Klavier (Unprinted)		
231	In der Heimath, PM	29.9.67	NW

158	Die Industriellen, W	19.1.64	Red
	(For the Industrial Societies' Ball)		
113	Irenen-Pf	23.8.61	NW
–	Iris, PM	2.61	
	(Unprinted, lost)		
–	Irrlichter, W	7.6.58	
	(Identical with Op. 218 by Johann Strauss?)		
–	Japanesischer Marsch	13.9.62	Pav
	(Appeared only in Russia)		
278	Jo[c]key, Ps	17.2.70	FH

| 216 | Jocus, Ps | 18.2.67 | DS |
| | (The artists' association, "Hesperus") | | |

23	Joujou, P	16.7.56	
27	Jucker-Polka	25.8.56	U
–	Jupiter und Pluto	29.12.61	
	(Musical farce in 30 scenes for 2 orchestras, in collaboration with Johann Strauss) (Partly existing)		
25	„Kadi"-Quadrille (A. Thomas)	16.9.56	VG
276	„Kakadu"-(„Vert-Vert") Qu (Offenbach)	3.70	
–	Klänge aus der Ober- und Unterwelt, Concertwalzer (Lost)	28.8.60	VG
70	Die'Kokette, Pf	5.59	
100	Die Kosende, PM	17.2.61	VG
59	Österreichischer Kronprinzen-Marsch	31.8.58	VG
	(The officers of the Crown Prince Rudolph Infantry Regt.) (In connection with the Prince's birth)		
226	Krönungslieder W	21.6.67	VG
	(See Ung. Krönungsmarsch)		

135	Künstler-Caprice, Pf	24.1.63	DS
	(The artists' association "Hesperus")		
274	Künstler-Gruß, Pf	15.1.70	MV
	(The Society of Friends of Music opening ball)		
–	Küsse mich, P. M.		
	(As Op. 122 published by Büttner in St. Petersburg)		
117	Die Lachtaube, PM	23.1.62	SBS
64	Lanciers-Quadrille	17.10.58	VG
60	Laxenburg-Polka	30.8.58	U
154	Lebensgeister, Pf	31.1.64	Red
	(Fürstin Eleonore von und zu Schwarzenberg)		
263	Mein Lebenslauf ist Lieb und Lust, W	7.2.69	Red
	(The students of Vienna)		

204	Die Libelle, PM	21.10.66	VG

56	Liebesgrüße, W	1.6.58	VG
–	Liebe und Leben, W	23.10.59	U
	(Unprinted, lost)		
122	Lieb und Wein, PM	17.6.62	Weg

36	Liechtenstein-Marsch	17.5.57	U
–	Lieder: (Songs)	49	
	1. Elegie (Jos. Strauß)		

2. Meineid (Jos. Strauß)
3. Der Totengräber (Jos. Strauß)
4. Nachtgebet (J.N. Vogl)
   (Autograph)
 – Lieder (Singly):
   „Der Bettler" (Otto Prechtler)
   (Autograph)
   „Wenn ein Kindlein" (Aug. Silberstein)
   (Österr. Volkskalender 1866)

| 233 | Lock-Polka | 5.1.68 | VG |

| 19 | Lust-Lager, P | 2.6.56 | BH |
| 91 | Lustschwärmer, W | 3.7.60 | VG |

17	Maiblümchen, PM	27.4.56	U
182	Mailust, Pf	25.5.65	NW
34	Mairosen, W	12.5.57	VG
–	Manövrir-Marsch	28.7.56	BH
244	Margherita, P	13.6.68	VG
	(For the wedding of Prince Humbert and		
	Princess Margherita)		
214	Marien-Klänge, W	10.2.67	Red
	(Fürstin Marie von Kinsky)		

202	Die Marketenderin, Pf	22.6.66	VG
–	Marketenderin vom Wienerwald, PM	25.5.59	GZ
	(Unprinted, lost)		

262	Neckerei, PM	8.2.69	FH
126	Neue-Welt-Bürger, W	27.7.62	NW
–	Neue-Welt-Polka	24.7.61	NW
	(Unprinted, lost)		
275	Nilfluthen, W	25.1.70	SBS
	("Concordia" ball on the theme, opening		
	of the Suez Canal)		

–	Nocturne	4.9.62	Pav
	(Lost)		
139	Normen, W	27.1.63	SBS
	(The law students)		
50	Nymphen-Polka	1.58	
271	Ohne Sorgen! Ps	22.9.69	Pav

45	Parade-Quadrille	18.8.57	VG
209	Pariser-Quadrille	1.67	DS
	(On songs of Dem. Teresa)		
–	Passiflora, PM	4.8.57	VG
	(Unprinted, lost)		
134	Patti-Polka („Lach-Polka")	15.3.63	VG
	(„Adelina Patti")		
190	Pauline, PM	28.1.66	SBS
	(„Pauline Fürstin Metternich")		

1.

2.

283   Rudolphsklänge, W   23.2.70   Red
       (The Students' Ball committee, patron:
       Crown Prince Rudolph)

22   Sehnsucht, PM   22.7.56   VG

Josef Strauss

125	Seraphinen-Pf	21.7.62	NW
–	Serenade (= Ständchen?)	9.62	Pav
	(Appeared only in Russia)		
40	La Simplicité, Pf	26.7.57	U
248	Die Sirene, PM	19.6.68	VG
68	Soll und Haben, W	19.1.59	SBS
	(Handels-Elite-Ball-Tänze)		
111	Die Sonderlinge, W	23.8.61	Weg
137	Sofien-Qu (On popular themes)		
	(For the name day of Archduchess Sofie)		
109	Die Soubrette, Ps	15.8.61	NW
140	Souvenir-Polka (On popular themes)	4.7.63	Sp
–	Souvenir à Patti, Potp.	10.12.65	VG
	(Unprinted, lost)		
235	Sphärenklänge, W	21.1.68	SBS
	(The medical students)		

192	Die Spinnerin, Pf	18.2.66	VG
170	Sport-Polka	9.10.64	DS
181	Springinsfeld, Ps	30.5.65	VG
–	Ständchen Nr. 1 (Orchester)	18.4.61	

43	Steeple ch(e)ase, P	31.8.57	U
80	Stegreif-Quadrille	15.7.59	VG
96	Sternschnuppen, W	27.8.60	U
183	Stiefmütterchen, PM	5.7.65	VG

| – | Stimmen aus der Zeit, W | 15.3.59 | VG |
| | (Unprinted, lost) | | |

Appendices

–	Strauß und Lanner, Potp.	1.1.65	VG
	(Unprinted)		
141	Streich-Magnete, W	9.2.63	SBS
	(The students of technology)		
222	Studententräume, W	25.2.67	Red
	(First performed at a students' ball in the "Redoutensaal")		
135	Sturmlauf, (Turner-) Ps	4.2.63	DS
	(The Vienna Gymnastics Club)		
75	Sturm-Polka	8.59	U
3	Sturm-Quadrille	19.8.55	

28	Sylphide, Pf	8.11.56	Sp
–	Sylvesterlieder, Potp.	31.12.65	DS
	(Unprinted, lost)		
73	Sympathie, PM	30.10.59	VG
93	Tag und Nacht, P	30.7.60	Sp

234	Tanzadresse an die Preisgekrönten, W	18.2.68	Red
	(The Association of Industrial Societies)		
266	Die tanzende Muse, PM	14.2.69	FH

227	Die Tänzerin, Pf	7.6.67	VG
120	Die Tanz-Interpellanten, W	25.2.62	SBS
280	Tanz-Prioritäten, W	6.2.70	Red
	(The Association of Industrial Societies)		
238	Tanz-Regulator, Pf	22.1.68	FH
6	Tarantel-Polka	12.8.55	U

| 195 | Thalia, PM
(The artists' association, "Hesperus") | 4.2.66 | DS |

213	Theater-Quadrille	12.1.67	DS
15	Titi-Polka	5.56	
265	„Toto"-Qu (J. Offenbach)	2.69	
130	Touristen-Qu (Incorporating popular folk-melodies)	26.12.62	VG
169	Tournier-Quadrille	17.8.64	NW
184	Transactionen, W	2.8.65	VG

–	Trifolien, W (In collaboration with Johann & Eduard Strauss, for the artists' association, "Hesperus")	13.2.65	DS
92	Turner-Quadrille („Den Turnern")	60	
225	Ungarischer Krönungsmarsch (Festival on the occasion of the coronation in Pest. (8.6.67) of the royal couple)	7.6.67	VG
–	Vaterländischer Marsch (In collaboration with Johann Strauss)	9.5.59	Sp
259	Vélocipède, Ps (= Fahrrad)	2.69	

198	Vereins-Lieder, W (The students of Vienna)	6.2.66	Red
2	Vergiß mein nicht, PM	12.8.55	U
185	Verliebte Augen, Pf	17.7.65	NW

29	Die Veteranen, W	18.11.56	Sp
	(On the occasion of the 90th birthday of		
	Field Marshal Radetzky)		
138	Victor-Marsch	13.5.63	VG
	(For the birthday of Archduke Ludwig		
	Victor)		
228	Victoria, Pf	27.6.67	
	(Festival in Hotel Victoria, Wieden)		

7	Vielliebchen, PM	55	
–	Vor der Schlacht, Chor	3.8.63	NW
	(Unprinted, lost)		
16	Die Vorgeiger, W	23.4.56	GZ
	(Josef Strauss; first appearance as violinist-leader)		
127	Vorwärts! Ps (= En avant!)	26.9.62	Pav
79	Waldbleamln, L	29.8.59	U

63	Waldröslein, PM	24.9.58	VG
41	Wallonen-Marsch	21.7.57	VG
	(On the occasion of the wedding of		
	Archduke Maximilian and Charlotte of		
	Belgium)		
18	Wiegenlieder, W (= Schlummerlieder)	15.7.56	VG
	(For the birth of Princess Gisella)		
–	Mein schönes Wien, Albumblatt		
	(Published in Berlin 1880)		
108	Wiener Bonmots, W	19.7.61	

–	Wiener Colibri, W	24.5.58	U
	(Unprinted, lost)		
150	Wiener Couplets, W	27.9.63	NW

| 249 | Wiener Fresken, W | 28.7.68 | VG |

–	Wiener-Garnison-Marsch	23.7.54	U
61	Wiener Kinder, W	17.8.58	VG
	(In Pawlowsk also „Heimathskinder")		

218	Wiener Leben, Pf	18.2.67	Schw
13	Wiener Polka	14.1.56	Schw
239	Wiener Stimmen, W	11.2.68	Red
	(The Citizens' Ball committee)		

| 104 | Aus dem Wienerwald, PM | 2.7.61 | Dom |
| 201 | Wilde Rose, PM | 29.7.66 | VG |

The compositions of Josef Strauss from Opus 1 to Op. 9, and from Op. 151 onwards were published by C.A. Spina; Op. 10 to Op. 150 by Carl Haslinger, both of Vienna.

Posthumous Arrangements of Music by Josef Strauss

Frühlingsluft, operetta in 3 acts, based on the French text of Carl Lindau and Julius Wilhelm. Music arranged by Ernst Reiterer from the works of Josef Strauss. Première: 9.5.1903 at "Venedig in Wien". Publisher: Doblinger, Vienna. Items published separately: Overture, Cake-walk, Knickebein March, Rosen Hochzeit waltz.

Frauenherz, operetta in 3 acts based on the French text of Carl Lindau. Music arranged by Ernst Reiterer from the works of Josef Strauss. Première: 29.9.1905 at Danzer's Orpheum, Vienna. Publisher: Doblinger, Vienna. Items published separately: Overture, Frauenherzen waltz, Leben and Geniessen waltz, Drillewitz March, American Quadrille, Concert scene – Ein Rätsel ist das Frauenherz (Woman's heart is a mystery).

Das Schwalberl aus dem Wienerwald, operetta in 3 acts and a prelude, by Emil Berger and Louis Taufstein. Music arranged by Fritz Sommer from the works of Josef Strauss. Première: 31.3.1906 at the Raimundtheater, Vienna. Publisher: Bard, Budapest.

Das Teufelsmädel, burlesque operetta by Josef Siegmund and Louis Taufstein. Music arranged by Ernst Siebert from the works of Josef Strauss. Première: 2.3.1908 at the Apollo Theater, Vienna. Publisher: Gustav Lewy, Vienna.

Die Weisse Fahne, operetta in 1 act by Fritz Grünbaum. Music arranged by Oscar Stalla from the works of Josef Strauss. Première: 17.11.1911 at the Cabaret "Die Hölle", Vienna.

Freut Euch des Lebens, operetta in 3 acts by Julius Wilhelm and Peter Herz. Music arranged by Bernhard Grün from the works of Johann and Josef Strauss. Première: 22.12.1932 at the Volksoper, Vienna. Publisher: Doblinger, Vienna.

Walzerträume, play with music, in 4 scenes, by Tilde Binder and Ernst Friese. Music arranged by Bruno Uher from the works of Josef Strauss. Première: 21.6.1942 at the Nuremberg Opera House – Viennese Première: 30.3.1943 at the Stadttheater. Publisher: Wiener Verlaganstalt.

Die Straussbuben, play with music, in 3 acts, by Hubert Marischka and Rudolf Weys. Music arranged by Oscar Stalla from the works of Johann and Josef Strauss. Première: 20.10.1946 at the Raimundtheater, Vienna. Item published separately: Overture. Publisher: Papageno-Musikverlag, Vienna.

Appendix 3

Register of Persons

THE FAMILY OF JOSEF STRAUSS

Johann, father	(1804–1849)
Anna Maria, mother	(1802–1870)
Johann, brother	(1825–1899)
Anna, sister	(1829–1903)
Therese, sister	(1831–1915)
Ferdinand, brother	(1834–1834)
Eduard (I), brother	(1835–1916)
Caroline, wife	(1831–1900)
Karoline, daughter	(1858–1919)
Jetty, sister-in-law	(1818–1878)
(Johann's wife)	
Marie, sister-in-law	(1840–1921)
(Eduard's wife)	
Eduard (II)	(1910–1969)
(grandson of Eduard I)	
Josephine Streim	(1808–1870)
(Aunt, married name Waber)	
Anna Streim	(1775–1863)
(Grandmother)	

ASSOCIATED CONTEMPORARIES

Fahrbach, Philipp	(1815–1885)
Haslinger, Carl	(1816–1868)
Lanner, August	(1834–1855)
Lanner, Joseph	(1801–1843)
Metternich, Pauline	(1836–1921)
Spina, C. A.	(1827–1906)
Trampusch, Emilie	(born 1814)
Weyl, Joseph	(1821–1895)
Ziehrer, C. M.	(1843–1922)

Appendix 4

Bibliography

Secondary literature about the Strauss family has been consciously disregarded. Apart from letters, documents and contemporary accounts, only the following sources were used:

Eduard Strauss: *Erinnerungen*, Vienna and Leipzig 1906 (Memoirs)

Max Schönherr/Karl Reinöhl: *Johann Strauss Vater*, Vienna 1954

Hanns Jäger-Sunstenau: *Der Walzerkönig und seine Dynastie*, Vienna 1965

Alexander Weinmann: *Sämtliche Werke von Johann Strauss Vater und Sohn*

Alexander Weinmann: *Sämtliche Werke von Josef und Eduard Strauss*, Vienna

Friedrich Haas: *Josef Strauss*, Fragmente einer Dissertation (Vienna City Library)

Max Schönherr: Articles in the *Oesterreichische Musikzeitschrift* (e.g. *Aesthetik des Walzers*)

John Whitten: *Johann Strauss und der Wiener Männergesang-Verein* (in the *Oesterreichische Musikzeitschrift* No. 10, 1975)

The author also wishes to thank:

Prof. Dr. Max Schönherr, for advice and assistance in revision;
Elizabeth Strauss, for providing the pictures and illustrations;
Hertha Brixler for providing Strauss family letters; and the eminent team of the Vienna City Library.

ILLUSTRATIONS

Illustrations are reproduced by kind permission of:

Historisches Museum der Stadt Wien
Wiener Stadtbibliothek
Handschriftensammlung der Wiener Stadtbibliothek
Musiksammlung der Wiener Stadtbibliothek
Bildarchiv der Österreichischen Nationalbibliothek
Archiv der Gesellschaft der Musikfreunde
Bilderdienst der Stadt Wien
Bildarchiv Preussischer Kulturbesitz, Berlin
Picture material on pages 12, 19, 21, 71 and 92 derives from
   private sources
Musical notation: Emmerich Fleissner.